SKISPOTS
ESPAC

Francis Jennen

Original concept by **Francis Johnston**
Original photography by the author, unless otherwise credited
Front cover photography courtesy of Salomon Sports, www. salomonsports.com

Produced by the Bridgewater Book Company
Project Editor: Emily Casey Bailey
Project Designer: Lisa McCormick

Published by Thomas Cook Publishing
PO Box 227, The Thomas Cook Business Park, Unit 15/16, Coningsby Road,
Peterborough PE3 8SB, United Kingdom
email: books@thomascook.com
www.thomascookpublishing.com
+44 (0) 1733 416477

First edition © 2005 Thomas Cook Publishing
Text © 2005 Thomas Cook Publishing
Maps © 2005 Thomas Cook Publishing
ISBN: 1-841575-11-9
Head of Thomas Cook Publishing: Chris Young
Project Editor: Kelly Anne Pipes
Production/DTP: Steven Collins

Snowsports and related activities have an inherent level of danger and carry
a risk of personal injury. They should be attempted only by those with a full
understanding of these risks and with the training/experience to evaluate them,
or under the personal supervision of suitably qualified instructors or mountain
guides. Mountain conditions are highly variable and change quickly – weather
and avalanche risk level conditions must be carefully considered.

ACKNOWLEDGEMENTS
This book is dedicated to Sofia Barbas and all my family. It is the result of many wonderful days and nights in the mountains, aided by and accompanied by some great characters. Specific thanks go to Jane Jacquemod and all the team at the Office du Tourisme, Val d'Isère; Jean-François Blas at Sofival; Jock and Susan Dun at Snowsports Business Enhancement; and Stéphanie Aillet and the team at Tignes Dévelopment and Corrine Raïh at the Agence Touristique Savoie.

CONTENTS

SYMBOLS KEY

The following is a key to the symbols used throughout this book:

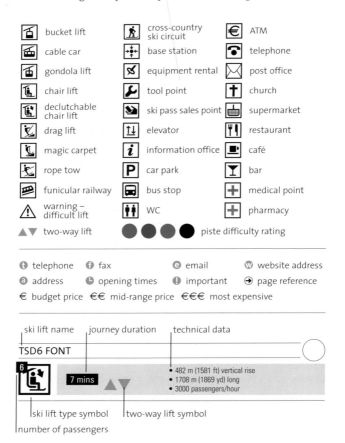

bucket lift	cross-country ski circuit	ATM
cable car	base station	telephone
gondola lift	equipment rental	post office
chair lift	tool point	church
declutchable chair lift	ski pass sales point	supermarket
drag lift	elevator	restaurant
magic carpet	information office	café
rope tow	car park	bar
funicular railway	bus stop	medical point
warning – difficult lift	WC	pharmacy
two-way lift	piste difficulty rating	

🕿 telephone   🕿 fax   @ email   W website address

@ address   🕘 opening times   ❶ important   ➔ page reference

€ budget price   €€ mid-range price   €€€ most expensive

---

ski lift name   journey duration   technical data

TSD6 FONT

| 6 | 7 mins ▲▼ | • 482 m (1581 ft) vertical rise
• 1708 m (1869 yd) long
• 3000 passengers/hour |

ski lift type symbol   two-way lift symbol

number of passengers

INTRODUCTION TO SKISPOTS

Welcome to SkiSpots, an innovative series of specialist guidebooks to Europe's top ski regions, designed and compiled by some of Europe's most experienced snowsports professionals. Whether you ski, board, blade or Langlauf, are a piste virgin or a seasoned powder hound, SkiSpots are as indispensable as your ski pass.

With a snowsports-centric layout and a snowsports-specific information flow, these guides are focused on the major linked ski domains and the resorts that access them: with historical snowfall charts and analysis as a guide to the best dates to visit for optimum snow conditions; base station layouts and resort street plans; detailed information and critiques on all principal ski lifts and pistes; ideas for alternative activities and après ski; and complemented by the history, culture, gastronomy, language and attractions of the surrounding region.

Action-packed and filled with insider intelligence and technical expertise, with a wealth of general information to keep non-skiers interested too, SkiSpots are the next best thing to having a private mountain guide.

On a piste map, the sun is always shining, the snow is always powder perfect, the visibility is always excellent and the links are always open. SkiSpots provide an invaluable extension to your piste map, describing the ski area in three dimensions, clarifying ambiguous and complicated routes, directing you away from the links that don't work and towards the areas that will deliver the most satisfying descents.

The author has visited every corner of the resorts and ski domains, taken and timed every lift, skied every piste and most of the powder fields in between and visited every recommended bar and restaurant – it's a dirty job, but someone's got to do it!

Snow excites a childlike fascination in us all; who hasn't felt the urge to rush out and throw a snowball after even the slightest frosting of this magical powder on a crisp winter morning? The first priority of this guidebook is to stimulate your excitement about the mountains, striving to inform and nourish your enjoyment of this wonderful environment and direct you to the best that the resorts and ski areas have to offer.

The first part of the book gives you a flavour of the region you are visiting, detailing the history of the area and the pioneering beginnings of the extensive snowsports infrastructure that you enjoy today; with an overview on the regional food and drink and a basic snowsports-centric vocabulary in the local language to help you engage more readily with your hosts and speed up assistance if and when you require it.

The second part of the guide begins with an all-important briefing on the dangers of the mountains in winter, and the tried and tested ways of minimizing the risks to which you expose yourself when participating in adventure sports in this environment; together with the rules and regulations that all slope users have to observe. Next comes the introduction to each major resort and ski area and how to access them; with street plans, piste maps and ski area data; ski pass information, resort transport, equipment hire, ski schools, childcare, resort and ski area services; plus snowfall history charts. Each sector of the ski area is then broken down by base station layout, first access points and onward links, with a detailed lift-by-lift description and piste-by-piste critique; every mountain bar and restaurant is covered in depth and suggested point-to-point itineraries are illustrated to assist with route planning to help you squeeze the maximum potential out of your day.

When the après-ski begins, SkiSpots continue with you by suggesting alternative activities and listing the cafés, restaurants, bars and clubs in which to round off your day. The book finishes with some ideas for days away from the pistes, together with an insight into the attractions of the region in summer.

www.ski-ride.com

Due to the ephemeral nature of snow, and the dynamic nature of the mountain environment and the snowsports industry, resort facilities and ski area boundaries can change. Therefore the SkiSpots series is also supported by an Internet portal, delivering up-to-the-minute news and links to the ski areas: on-site webcams, live snow reports and current weather information, resort fact sheets, events diary, tour operator links and much more, enhancing both this guidebook and your trip.

HOW TO USE THIS BOOK

SkiSpots travel guides give ski lift and piste information in a unique graphical format. Detailed information is given on the type of ski lift, journey duration, capacity, directions to follow on arrival and onward links. All principal pistes are covered: colour-coded by level of difficulty and detailing access routes, descriptions of terrain, best lines of descent and onward links, accompanied by regular piste map illustrations to help you in real-time itinerary planning and route-finding on-the-move.

Point-to-point route-finder information is not necessarily the quickest option, but rather the best on-piste direction to deliver the most enjoyable route between the specified points. The route-finders are detailed for both competent novices and good intermediates.

ABOUT THE AUTHOR

Francis (Gary) Johnston was born in County Down, Northern Ireland. He was previously employed at a senior level with two of the UK's leading Ski, Lakes & Mountains tour operators, having lived and worked in Andorra, Spain and Portugal. He has also worked in or visited most of the leading French, Austrian and Italian ski resorts, having personally accompanied and guided well over four thousand visitors and travel industry professionals during that time.

Francis now divides his time between Andorra, France and Brighton in England; travelling up to six months each year in the Alps and Pyrenees.

❶ The Alpine environment can be harsh and dangerous, but it is also very fragile – please respect it and leave nothing but your tracks in the snow.

WELCOME – BIENVENUE

The Espace Killy is one of snowsport's most mythical destinations, home to some of Europe's most extensive and most exciting ski terrain. It is the collective name for the combined ski areas of Val d'Isère and Tignes, which have been joined together since 1971 to form one of the world's largest lift- and piste-linked ski domains. The two resorts share the same mountains, but present two contrasting faces and provide two very different holiday experiences: Val d'Isère, with its more traditional character, upmarket ambiance and more human scale; and Tignes, with its huge futuristic apartment edifices, stark above-the-treeline landscape and ski-to-door convenience.

The area is situated at the top end of the Tarentaise Valley, in France's historically important and once independent Savoie region, on the rugged natural frontier with Italy and at the gateway to France's premier national park, the wild and beautiful Vanoise. The Tarentaise is a snowsports super-region, and the drive up to the Espace Killy passes the road junctions for some of the world's other biggest names in snowsports, such as the Trois Vallées and Paradiski. What inspires the snowsports cognoscenti to pass these by and continue on to the roof of the valley? Part of the answer is in the question: as the highest resorts in the region, both Val d'Isère and Tignes are blessed with favourable micro-climates that endow their slopes with the best quality snow; their high altitude setting also means that the abundant quantity of snow lasts longer once fallen. Both resorts have access to glacial zones that permit skiing even during the summer, with Tignes open for skiing during all four seasons.

◀ *Village chair lift at Val d'Isère*

STATISTICS
- Seven major Alpine mountains
- Altitude: min 1550 m (5086 ft), max 3456 m (11,339 ft)
- Vertical drop: 1906 m (6254 ft)
- Ski area: 131 pistes, extending to 300 km (186 miles) in length
- Further info: www.valdisere.com and www.ski-tignes.com

CUTTING EDGE

With such an expansive territory, there's something for everyone – nervous novices or experienced adrenaline junkies. However, the prime attraction is definitely the technical difficulty of the accessible terrain, with some of the most exhilarating lift-served off-piste in Europe. Both resorts are firmly at the vanguard of 'new school' snowsports and the exceptional Naturides and Tignes' novel Le SPOT area are perfect examples of this ethos: lift-served slopes and side valleys where all descents are within the ski area and protected by the piste security services, but left as ungroomed 'natural' powder fields where the only limits are those you set yourself.

The area has witnessed some of France's, and so the world's, defining snowsports moments: a Val d'Isère local was (at St Moritz in 1948) the first French skier to win a Winter Olympic gold medal; the French National Ski School was conceived on these slopes; and Tignes was a pioneer of the concept of the ski-in/ski-out resort. This tradition of excellence continues today and the area is home to world-beaters such as Ingrid Jacquemod, Guerlain Chicherit and Nicolas Huet.

Come share in the experience that has produced these champions and set the benchmark for snowsports excellence.

REGIONAL IDENTITY

The Celtic and Gallic tribes that were the earliest settled inhabitants of these harsh Alpine valleys gradually succumbed to the rise and expansion of the Roman Empire from 121 BC. The Romans permitted compliant Burgundian tribes from the Rhine Valley to resettle the upland valleys and the area began to develop as a defined region. After the fall of the Roman Empire, the region became part of the kingdom of Burgundy and was subject to frequent changes of fortune following various conflicts during the next five centuries. Burgundy was eventually incorporated into the Holy Roman Empire in 1032 and the Burgundian ruler, Humbert I (c.980–1048, known as 'white hands') was awarded the territories that were to become Savoie, in recognition of his acceptance of the sovereignty of Emperor Conrad II. He took the title of Count and founded the House of Savoie. Over the next five centuries, Humbert's successors made skilled alliances with neighbouring states, consolidating Savoie's advantageous position as 'gatekeeper' of the Alps to become a major player in European politics. Under the guidance of Count Amadeus VIII (reigned 1391–1440) who was eventually made a duke of the Holy Roman Empire, Savoie's dominions stretched from Geneva to Nice and included the neighbouring regions of Val d'Aosta and Piedmont in modern-day Italy.

Conflict with France precipitated the move of Savoie's capital from Chambéry to Turin in 1563 and over the next two hundred years this strategic border region became a key bargaining territory in all major power struggles in central Europe. It suffered from both Spanish and French occupation before it was eventually returned to the House of Savoie, which by then had gained royal status with the kingdom of Sardinia.

In 1789, the storming of the Bastille marked the start of the French Revolution and in 1792 Savoie was occupied by revolutionary forces and annexed to France. Following Napoleon's defeat at Waterloo, Savoie was returned to the Sardinian monarchy, where it remained until ceded, along with Nice, to Napoleon III in 1858, in return for a French alliance against the Austrians to help reunite Italy. The French Republic granted the Savoyards a plebiscite, the vote unanimously favoured union with France and the territory was divided into two *départements*, Savoie and Haute-Savoie, corresponding to the present-day areas. Thus ended over eight hundred years of autonomous Savoie history, as the House of Savoie sacrificed the land of their forbears for the crown of Italy and the subjects of Savoie became citizens of France. Only with the abdication of Italy's last king, Humbert II, in 1946, did the rule of the House of Savoie finally come to an end, a dynasty that had lasted almost a millennium.

TOWARDS THE PRESENT DAY

During World War II, the Resistance was particularly active through-out the two Savoies, securing the liberation of the region in August 1945. But the reprisals and destruction from the Nazi occupation had a terrible effect on the region, and it was left economically and demographically weakened. Following the war, the Alpine foothills and fertile river valleys were re-established as important agricultural areas, specializing in dairy products and fruit cultiva-tion. The biggest factors in the redevelopment of the region were the establishment of major hydroelectric plants and the rapidly growing mountain tourist industry, which secured Savoie's return to the world stage as an important economic powerhouse, this time subject to the forces of nature and ruled by the seasons.

VAL D'ISÈRE

Official records date Val d'Isère from the 16th century; the village was previously known as l'Aval de Tignes, a small hamlet huddled around its church at the end of a single mule track, cut off from the lower Tarentaise Valley for almost eight months of the year. The inhabitants, still referred to locally today as Avalins, created lacework and cheeses to take on the long and often perilous trek down to Bourg-St-Maurice to barter and sell at the town's market. Gradually, the better opportunities and easier life of the more modern lowland towns and cities drew most of the younger inhabitants away to escape the harsh mountain life. Then, in the 1930s, a remarkable reversal of fortunes changed the dynamics of this almost forgotten high altitude valley: the newly fashionable sport of skiing altered perceptions of the once negative climatic conditions and now became one of the area's most valuable assets. The long winter season, bountiful snowfalls and ideal orientation of the surrounding slopes helped Val d'Isère establish itself as one of Europe's most favourable wintersports stations; emigration declined and the almost lost hamlet, now renamed as the village of Val d'Isère, began an impressive renaissance. Three central figures drove the initial development of the station: Charles Diebold, Jacques Mouflier and Nicolas Bazile. Charles Diebold was one of the pioneers of the French national ski and mountaineering school, establishing the first ski school in 1932; Jacques Mouflier built the first ski lift, the Rogoney lift, in 1934; and Nicolas Bazile, who had been elected Mayor in 1927, founded and presided over Val d'Isère's first tourist office.

World War II intervened in the area's progress, but the newly created Val d'Isère lift company (STVI – Société des Téléphériques de Val d'Isère) kept an eye on the future and illicitly began construction of the Solaise cable car in 1940, right under the noses of the occupying forces. Access to the village had been aided by the prewar construction of the Col de l'Iseran road, providing a more constant influx of visitors and helping Val d'Isère grow in stature on the international snowsports scene during the prosperous postwar years. Now with town status, this ever-burgeoning wintersports station became forever associated with skiing excellence when Henri Oreiller, the son of a local baker, became France's first Olympic gold medalist for skiing at the 2nd Winter Olympics at St Moritz in 1948. Other local heros also flew the flag for the region: Marielle Goitschel took the gold medal at the World Championships in Chamonix in 1962, and the town's proudest moment was local boy Jean-Claude Killy's triple gold grand slam at the 1968 Grenoble Winter Olympics, a feat that still resonates in the prestige of the station. Following the agreement to link Val d'Isère's ski area with that of Tignes in 1971, the huge combined ski domain was eventually named after Killy in recognition of his championing of the Tarentaise region and his part in securing the return of the Winter Olympics, this time to Albertville, in 1992; with Val d'Isère hosting the men's blue riband skiing events on the Face de Bellevarde.

Now well into its eighth decade as a major sports and tourism station, the town continues to strengthen its position in both snowsports and summer tourism, constantly upgrading its facilities and infrastructure to keep pace with the demands of an increasingly competitive industry. It secured the right to host the 2009 World Alpine Skiing Championships, and continues to attract the snowsports spotlight. The Avalin heart still beats softly at the core of the old village, but Val d'Isère marches proudly into the future as one of snowsports' most emblematic stations.

TIGNES

The story of Tignes is one of destruction and rebirth. The original village of Tignes nestled at the bottom of the valley on the banks of the Isère River at 1550 m (5086 ft); it had a few small summer-only hotels, but mostly abided to the seasonal rhythm of Alpine agriculture. In 1860, the village was visited by William Mathews, one of the founders of the Alpine Club of Great Britain, who made Tignes his base for a series of first conquests on a bevy of the major peaks in the area, including la Grande Casse and la Grande Sassière. Following Mathews' exploits, the area soon became a popular base camp for Alpinists and grew to accommodate the influx of adventurous tourists, eventually boasting ten hotels. In 1925, the first chalet was built at the high altitude meadows on the shores of the lake at 2100 m (6890 ft), followed by a hotel in 1932. In 1934, the first ski school was founded and in 1936 the first ski lift was constructed, marking the first real steps in the creation of the resort.

The true birth of Tignes 2100, however, was a forced labour. Following WWII, the reconstruction of France became a priority and various Grands Projects were announced to help rebuild the nation. These projects included the harnessing of the tremendous natural energy of the Alpine torrents to provide hydroelectric power, and the summer of 1947 sounded the death knell for Tignes as construction began on the huge dam on the Isère River, just below the village. In 1952, a year still remembered as the *année terrible* by present-day Tignards, the dam was completed and the sluice gates were closed. As the waters rose to create the new Lac du Chevril reservoir, the original Tignes village slowly disappeared beneath the deluge and its inhabitants dispersed throughout the Tarentaise.

Tignes' community spirit wasn't completely extinguished however, and in 1954 a group of forward-thinking pioneers began a project that would see Tignes reborn as a modern high-altitude sports station. The modernist architect Raymond Pantz was commissioned to design a resort village that would allow Tignes 2100 to establish itself as a major player in snowsports tourism. The massive curved edifice of le Bec Rouge at Tignes-le-Lac is the product of that initiative, with the sweeping structure designed to make the most of the views over the lake and the mountains beyond. In the 1970s, the property developer Pierre Schnebelen put forward the revolutionary idea of a ski-in/ski-out resort, where skiers could access ski lifts immediately outside their accommodation and return on-piste to their door at the end of the day. Tignes' Val Claret was born out of that original vision and quickly became the benchmark for this new convenient design of ski resort which, along with a concurrent and equally ingenious project to construct ski lifts on the glacier at la Grande Motte, put Tignes squarely on the Alpine map once again.

Since 1994, a new impetus has driven the resort's development: the fashion for futuristic architectural statements has waned and a more environmentally aware movement has directed initiatives, such as the provision of underground car parks to decrease congestion in the resort, allowing the reclamation of a central communal space in front of the Maison de Tignes-le-Lac and an increased pedestrian-friendly focus. The construction of the Grande Motte funicular tube train in 1993 was the apogee of the reconstruction of Tignes; the town has physically and culturally come a long way from its roots as an Alpine valley village to its position today as a major high-altitude resort at the cutting edge of Alpine sports.

▲ *The 'Giant of Tignes' mural on the Barrage de Tignes*

ESPACE PATRIMOINE

The history of Tignes and its environs is well recorded and presented in a permanent exhibition at a museum at the Maison de Tignes-le-Lac tourist information centre, with photographs, eye-witness accounts, films and artefacts chronicling the trans-formation and progress of the community over seven centuries. The exhibition also features fascinating insights into the construction of the ski lifts, including samples of the cables and data regarding the astronomical lengths and weights of metal utilized. Video headsets showing a series of 3-D films on major periods of development for the ski station are another key feature. All information is translated into English.

The Maison de Tignes-le-Lac is centrally located above the main bus/coach station, at the base of the Palafour and Millonex ski lifts and just a short stroll from the Aeroski gondola.

◐ Museum opening hours: Sun–Fri 16.00–19.00 hours; small admission charge. ☎ +33 (0)4 79 40 04 40

FOOD & DRINK
Gastronomy

● *Savoyard specialities are widely available in resort restaurants*

TRADITIONAL SAVOIE FARE

Regional gastronomy has too often been regarded as of secondary importance in the snowsports holiday experience. However, more discerning travellers are now seeking to complement their time in the mountains with great meals too. The rich diversity of European regional cuisine is nowhere more enjoyable than in the actual regions that created it.

France consistently lives up to its reputation as the world's foremost provider of gourmet food and fine wines and you could read an entire library of books on French gastronomy alone, not to mention the rich cuisine of the neighbouring Italian regions. Narrowing the focus to the specialities of Savoie should give you sufficient flavour of the rich tradition of high mountain cooking that is alive and well in this region.

With very little mountain land area suitable for intensive farming, surviving the harsh high-altitude winters through history required a rustic, hearty diet that made full use of the limited range of indigenous foodstuffs. Savoie mountain cuisine was therefore born out of necessity, relying heavily on dairy products from cows, goats and sheep; meat; game; a few hardy fruit and vegetable crops; together with foodstuffs harvested during the months of summer and autumn and preserved either by curing, drying or bottling.

REGIONAL PRODUCE

chou: Savoy cabbage; the most renowned vegetable from the region and a real staple of the Savoyard diet

coings: quinces; acidic pear-shaped fruit. These are popular mountain fruits because they are quite hardy and flourish where softer fruit would struggle; an important source of Vitamin C in a mountain diet and used to make preserves and desserts such as rissoles – quince paste spread on fingers of cornmeal and then baked or deep fried, served warm sprinkled with sugar

framboises, mûres and airelles: raspberries, blackberries and bilberries; these are available for very short seasons. At the turn of the 20th century, when phylloxera wiped out much of the region's vines, many vineyards were replanted with raspberries and production is still very prevalent today, particularly in the lakes area around Aix-les-Bains and Annecy

noix: walnuts; raw, in salads, pressed for walnut oil and even distilled into a liqueur, walnuts are an emblematic fruit of the Savoie and Isère *départements*

pommes: apples – Golden Delicious, Jonagold, Elstar, Melrose and Idared are the most common amongst the dozen or so preferred varieties of the region. The fresh fruit and juice carry an *Indication Géographique Protégée* (IGP) label protected by European Commission law and guaranteeing provenance from particular regions

pommes de terre: potatoes; a staple of the Savoie diet ever since they were introduced into the Duchy from its Italian territories, long before Savoie was a part of France

poires: pears – Conference, Williams and Général Leclerc are the three most common and easily recognized varieties of the half-a-dozen regional favourites; they also have an IGP label

QUALITY GUARANTEES
Indication Géographique Protégée (IGP): established by the European Commission to protect geographic names applied to agricultural products, such as Savoie apples and pears.
Label Régional Savoie: a guarantee of provenance from the Savoie region and, by association, a guarantee of quality.
Appellation d'Origine Contrôlée (AOC): official provenance and quality guarantee protected by EC law. AOC recognizes and protects the specific characteristics inherent in regional produce as an original blend of geographic position, reputation, tradition and knowledge passed down the generations, producing a unique set of circumstances which impart a peculiar quality to the product. Corresponds to the Europe-wide *Appellation d'Origine Protégée* (AOP), protected designation of origin law.

DAIRY PRODUCTS

Dairy herds play a major part in the gastronomic heritage of Savoie, and their produce brims with the flavour and goodness of this pure environment. Alpine-specific breeds of cattle, mostly Abondance and Tarine, are pastured on the high altitude meadows during the short Alpine summer from mid-June to early September.

Chevrotin goats have been farmed here since the 17th century and their cheese carries an AOC. Like the cattle, the goats are subject to a transhumance (transfer) every spring to the high altitude meadows, though the goats range much further and higher. The animals are milked twice a day and the cheese-making process is still mainly carried out by hand on-site in high altitude barns.

CHEESES

Reblochon AOC: strong-smelling soft cheese made with milk from Abondance cattle, which is pressed into hand-sized rounds and is one of the prime ingredients of *tartiflette* (see page 31). Traditionally made from the sweeter second milking (the *rebloche*)

Beaufort AOC: the 'Prince of Gruyères': a strong hard cheese moulded into large rounds using beechwood hoops, which not only maintain the shape but also give the cheese its distinctive concave edge. It has a delicate ivory colour but strong flavour. Used in *fondue Savoyarde* and in gratin dishes

Tomme de Savoie: A medium-hard cheese with small holes and a rich creamy taste (awarded a Savoie label). In the Savoyard dialect, the word *Tomme* simply means 'cheese', but also refers to the mould in which the cheeses are pressed

Tome des Bauges AOC: unpasteurized cow's milk cheese that has the same roots as Tomme de Savoie but a little stronger and firmer. Originates from the protected Bauges massif north-east of Chambéry

Emmental de Savoie: cow's milk cheese with a rich, creamy interior and smooth with well-distributed holes. Traditionally ripened for 75 days (awarded a Savoie label)

Chevrotin AOC: goat's milk cheese mostly from the Aravis area of Haute-Savoie, around the ski resort of La Clusaz. Exclusively produced on individual farms, not collectives

Tamié: fine cow's milk cheese produced by Trappist monks near Albertville; its packaging is instantly recognizable as it bears the Maltese cross

Bleu de Tignes: the ski resort's own small blue-veined, cow's milk cheese; a speciality of *La Ferme des 3 Capucines* at Le Lavachet, Tignes-le-Lac

CURED MEATS & SAUSAGES

Ham (*jambon*) and cured sausages (*salaisons*) are staples of the Alpine diet because they are an excellent way to preserve meat for the long winters. *Jambon de Savoie* is salted, dry-cured and aged for 9–12 months. Also try the lamb hams from the area around the resort of Valloire.

◉ *Market stall at Tignes*

There seem to be as many varieties of cured sausage in Savoie as there are cheeses in France! Savoie dry sausages are always made with natural casings, slowly aged and never frozen. They are served as starters, in salads and stews. The most popular include:

pormoniers de Tarentaise: pork offal with leeks and herbs
diots: small fresh meat sausage, either pork or pork and beef. Normally cooked in white wine
caïon: in the Savoyard dialect *caïon* means pig; in traditional Savoyard restaurants the word may signify regional pork sausages
saucissons d'âne: sausages made with donkey meat
salaisons de Savoie: *salaisons* is simply a generic name for charcuterie, taken here to signify specialities from Savoie

FISH

The clear, pure mountain rivers and lakes provide an important source of protein in the Alpine diet. The largest lakes are now protected and strictly controlled to minimize pollution.
char: delicate and succulent fish common in the lakes, particularly Lac d'Annecy; a regional delicacy throughout Savoie

lavaret and féra: commonly encountered as 'whitefish' on English menu translations. Both are the same species (dace) but differently named to distinguish the *lavaret* as the variety from the Lac du Bourget or Lac d'Annecy, and *féra* from Lac Léman. Generally served *à la meuniere* (see page 28) or in a light cream sauce

truite: trout; fresh river trout, rather than farmed, is the most prized and is stipulated as such on the menu

omble chevalier: member of the salmon family, similar to rainbow trout, which lives in deep, cold glacial lakes. A less common, much prized fish with an excellent flavour

VEGETARIAN

It has to be said, vegetarians will have a hard time of it in the mountains, vegans even more so. The concept of vegetarianism still isn't fully understood, or acceptably accommodated, even in the largest hotels. You may have to resign yourself to picking through salads and pizzas to remove anchovies, prawns and ham.

Most of the vegetarian options offered depend heavily on salads, eggs and cheese, with the omelette being king. Buffets and self-service restaurants are easiest, but they still rely on meat and fish dishes for main courses; the only vegetarian option again usually being an omelette – charged at the same price as the meat dish.

Crêpes, pasta and pizzas are reliable options; raclette and fondue are the best regional specialities for vegetarians (see page 31).

COOKING TECHNIQUES

Savoyard recipes have been influenced by the techniques and ingredients assimilated from the neighbouring French regions of Lyonnais, Bresse and Dauphiné, the Italian regions of Val d'Aosta and Piedmont (once ruled by Savoie), and wisps from the Mediterranean, too. The following are a selection of the most popular and representative styles:

à la meunière: dipped in flour and fried in butter

au gratin: with grated cheese and often breadcrumbs, as in *gratin de pommes de terre Savoyard* (fine slices of potato and grated Beaufort cheese oven baked with butter and stock to produce a rich, creamy energy-rich dish)

à la bergère: 'shepherd style', generally meaning with ham, mushrooms, onion and very finely cut potatoes

à la bourguignonne: 'Burgundy style', generally meaning casseroled with red wine, onions and mushrooms, but also frequently encountered as a style of fondue where meat is dipped in hot oil instead of the Savoie style where hot cheese is the dipping mix. A *fondue bourguignonne* includes a selection of sauces in which to dip the cooked meat, mainly curried mayonnaise and tomato salsa

à l'italienne: using pasta and tomatoes

à l'ancienne: prepared to an old, very traditional recipe; used as a generic term with no set ingredients or method of cooking

à la lyonnaise: 'Lyon style', cooked with onions. Usually encountered as a potato dish

à la niçoise: 'Nice style', usually applied to salad or pizza and including anchovies, tomatoes and olives in the ingredients; with French beans and egg too when referring to the salad.

à la vigneron: 'wine grower style', generally any recipe involving wine in its key ingredients

à la crème: made with cream; that is, in a cream sauce

à la dauphinoise: potatoes baked in cream/milk, usually served *au gratin*. A speciality of the neighbouring Isère region

WELL DONE

The French prefer meat rare (*bleu or saignante*), so if you prefer it to be well done (*bien cuit*) try asking for it to be very well done (*très bien cuit*), otherwise it is likely to arrive closer to medium (*à point*).

LOCAL DISHES

A noble culinary heritage pervades the kitchens and restaurants here and Savoie's tongue-twisting, tastebud-teasing fare, redolent of the rigours and pleasures of high altitude life, positively thrives.

tartiflette: ubiquitous staple of Savoie chalet kitchens, served for lunch and/or dinner. Sliced potatoes, Reblochon cheese, lardons, butter, onions, garlic and crème fraîche; oven baked and served almost bubbling. Traditionally served with charcuterie and pickles

raclette: a half-wheel of smooth, firm raclette cheese served on a special little heater to melt the cheese, which you scrape off hot on to your plate or bread. Usually served with potatoes and pickles

fondue: in Savoie, usually the cheese version. *Fondue savoyarde* is a blend of two or more cheeses and white wine, gently brought to near boiling to liquify, then served in a pot with a flame burner to keep it hot. Using little spears, you dip chunks of bread into the bubbling cheese. Usually served with potatoes and/or salad and charcuterie. If you're vegetarian, be sure to order the cheese version, not the meat-based one (*fondue bourguignonne*)

pierrade: small strips of meat cooked on a hot slate sprinkled with rock salt, usually a DIY task at your table; served with dips and salad

potée savoyarde: stew, usually ham and including Savoy cabbage and potatoes, served with the broth poured over toasted bread

polenta: made from milled corn and normally associated with the neighbouring Italian regions of Val d'Aosta and Piedmont, but in fact an ancient and important Savoie speciality. It is easy to store and used in many dishes as an important source of energy during the long winter; traditionally served with sausages or meat in sauce

crozets: Savoyard pasta. Tiny squares of wheat pasta, sometimes blended with buckwheat flour (*crozets au sarrasin*)

MENU

To see the menu, ask for *la carte*, because the 'menu' in France is taken to mean the daily set menu.

Menu du jour: an economical set menu, usually two or three courses, with at least two choices; often with dessert, bread and sometimes even water and/or table wine included.

MOUNTAIN SPORTS NUTRITION

Don't make the mistake of regarding eating on snowsports' holidays as merely pit-stops for refuelling: a couple of beers and a hamburger won't help you nail that three-sixty or give you the legs to progress into that fresh powder after lunch!

Nutritious, warming meals with quality, fresh ingredients and frequent non-alcoholic fluid intake are what your body craves at altitude. Remember, you are in an Arctic environment participating in a demanding sport. This requires an athletic-minded approach to diet. Far better to supply your body with optimum nutrition while, since you're on holiday, allowing yourself a more gourmet event. If you had a racehorse worth millions, you wouldn't feed it beer and hamburgers! So why treat yourself as any less worthy?

SUGGESTED SNOWSPORTS DIET

Breakfast: a 'Continental' breakfast of coffee, croissant and cigarette just isn't adequate to support a morning in the mountains. You need slow-release energy-rich foods such as muesli, bread with cheese or ham, honey and yogurt.

Lunch: light, warm dishes based on pasta, rice or vegetables with meat or fish to supply plenty of complex carbohydrate energy, protein and fibre.

Dinner: salad, soup or vegetables, followed by fish, fowl or light meat. Don't make it too hearty because a heavy meal will interfere with your sleep.

Snacks: fruit or yogurt or a sandwich or dried fruits/nuts.

Drinks: fruit juice, tea (herbal is best), hot chocolate, water and more water.

WINE

A giant in the oenological world, France needs no preamble regarding the quality of its wines. The Savoie region has been producing wines since Roman times and they were referred to by Pliny (23–79AD), who named them as the wines of Allobrogie; *vin de pays d'Allobrogie* is now the name used for good-quality table wines produced outside the AOC boundaries.

The rich alluvial land of the Combe de Savoie boasts a number of excellent, yet relatively little-known wines. Mostly subtle whites, they should be drunk young and go very well with the delicate lake fish and creamy local cheeses. They are also used extensively in cooking, featuring as a key ingredient in *fondue savoyarde* (see page 31) to help liquefy the cheese.

FRENCH WINE TERMS

Appellation d'Origine Contrôlée (AOC): the premier quality control, protected by law, awarded to the highest quality wines in specifically demarcated areas

Vin Délimité de Qualité Supérieure (VDQS): quality award just below full AOC

Vin de Pays: followed by the name of the *département* from which it comes. Local table wine

Vin Doux Naturel (VDN): naturally sweet wine (dessert wine).

cru: there are two distinct meanings to this term: it can refer to the specific territory where the wine originates, but is also used as a standard of classification normally encountered with champagnes and fine wines, which take the terms Premier Cru, Grand Cru and Premier Grand Cru, denoting the very highest quality

sec: dry; **moëlleux**: sweet; **pétillant** (or **perlé**): slightly sparkling; **mousseux**: sparkling; **crémant**: a gentler, 'foaming' version

There are currently just over 2000 ha (4942 acres) of vineyards in Savoie, located on mountain foothills, valleys and lake shores. There are four principal AOCs (Vin de Savoie; Roussette de Savoie; Crépy; and, the oldest, Seyssel, first awarded in 1942) and 22 Crus. All have the distinctive cross of Savoie moulded just below the neck of the bottle. The Vin de Savoie AOC is subdivided into Abymes, Apremont, Arbin, Ayze, Bergeron, Chautagne, Chignin, Cruet, Jongieux, Marignan, Marin, Montmélian, Ripaille, St Jean de la Porte, St Jeoire Prieuré and Pétillant de Savoie. The Roussette de Savoie AOC is subdivided into Frangy, Marestel, Monterminod and Monthoux.

No fewer than twenty-three different varieties of grape are cultivated; three times more whites than reds, as the whites are best suited to the chalky soil. Varieties grown include:

WHITES

Jacquère: predominates in the Combe de Savoie and Les Abymes areas, used in Apremont and Abymes wines. Light dry white, with a very delicate yellow tint

Bergeron: almost exclusively grown in the Chignin Cru communes

Altesse: most common in Seyssel and Frangy and used in AOC Roussette de Savoie. Legend has it that a Cypriot royal introduced this variety from her homeland on her visit to Savoie

Chasselas: mainly grown in the regions nearest the Swiss border

Roussanne: predominantly cultivated in the Chignin Cru

REDS

Mondeuse: the most prevalent Savoie red, mostly grown in the Combe de Savoie. Makes wines with a rich purple-red hue, and a bouquet of strawberry, raspberry and violet. Good with charcuterie

Pinot Noir: some used in the Chignin Vin de Savoie reds

Gamay: classic old-world grape cultivated for its reliability

VIN CHAUD

A hot mulled wine, which is an ubiquitous après-ski warmer in Alpine ski resorts.

Recipe: *1 bottle (75 cl) red Vin de Savoie, 115 g (4 oz) sugar, 1 thinly sliced lemon, thyme, bay leaf, clove.*

Heat the wine and sugar in a saucepan. When the froth begins to form, remove pan from the heat and add the lemon slices and other ingredients. Return to the heat and allow to boil for no more than two minutes. Serve hot.

APERITIFS & DIGESTIFS

génépy: a generic term for all Savoie spirits using Alpine wormwood in their flavouring. The liqueur is served as an aperitif and/or digestif and is often used in Savoie to flavour pastries and desserts

absinthe: potent, mind-altering, and once banned. Based on Alpine wormwood and believed to help relieve altitude sickness, although you probably just forget you have it!

vermouth: the Dolin label in Chambéry is a local producer of a fine AOC Vermouth. Based on a dry white Vin de Savoie and made to a secret recipe of orange essence, berries, Alpine flowers and herbs

marc de Savoie: Savoie brandy, often based on a pear wine

antésite: a non-alcoholic concentrate of liquorice, which you add to mineral water. First introduced over a century ago by a pharmacist from Voiron, south-west of Chambéry, and used to aid digestion

⬤ *Virtually every village has its own version of* génépy

LIGHTER DRINKS

bière: beer. Most of the beers available in resort bars are standard international brews sold from the tap. However, there is one brand with stronger local connections – the Brasserie de Cimes is a notable local producer from Aix-les-Bains; look out for their strong Piste Noire and Bâton de Feu beer, the white beer Aiguille Blanche and a super-strength (8 per cent) Yeti lager

café: coffee; with breakfast, or even just as breakfast, as a mid-morning or afternoon pick-me-up, after dinner and at just about any other social encounter, a coffee is as much of a national institution in France as 'a nice cup of tea' is in the UK. The variations in preference are wide ranging: **décaféiné** is decaf; **café crème** is made with milk or cream and is more commonly referred to as **café au lait**; **café noir** is a small black coffee; **café express** is espresso. *Café crème/café au lait* is traditionally drunk only at breakfast by the French, but at any time of day by tourists

tisane: a herbal infusion; this is the generic term in French for any herbal tea

eau: water. The Alps have a plethora of natural springs, which are the source of many brands of bottled water. Most comes from the Haute-Savoie, from springs at the foot of the Alps on the southern shores of Lac Léman, but bottled water from the spa town of Aix-les-Bains on the shores of Lac du Bourget is an excellent local mineral water. There are various types of water to choose from: *eau gazeuse* refers to sparkling water; *eau plate* is still; *eau nature* is plain tap water; and *eau minérale* is mineral water, such as Perrier or Evian, each from a specific source and high in mineral content – and often with quite a distinct, even salty, taste.

Although tap water quality is generally excellent, it is best to drink only bottled water.

DELICATESSENS & GOURMET SHOPS

Ferme de l'Adroit Farm restaurant and shop selling their own cheeses and speciality breads. ⓐ Just outside Val d'Isère, in the direction of Le Laisinant

Maison Gourmand Fine wines, including vin de Savoie, charcuterie, honey, preserves. ⓐ Central Val d'Isère (opposite the tourist office)

Maison Chevallot An unmissable pâtisserie/café in the Val Village shopping area. Massive range of speciality breads, tarts and cakes, chocolates and ice cream, all made in-house at this award-winning confectioners. ⓐ Central Val d'Isère (opposite the post office)

Chez le Pôvre Mimi Lovely delicatessen with high-quality Savoyard gourmet foods and regional specialities. ⓐ Avenue Olympique, Val d'Isère (the high street, facing the hotel Tsanteleina)

Le Chalet du Pain Huge range of speciality breads, pastries, cakes and confectionery. Hand-made ice-creams too. ⓐ Promenade de Tovière, Tignes-le-Lac le Rosset; and Hameau le Borsat, Val Claret (near Club Med)

Les Celliers Wide range of vins de Savoie, regional liqueurs, charcuterie and ready-made raclettes and fondues to take away; fondue sets and raclette heaters available to loan. ⓐ Gallerie du Palafour, Tignes-le-Lac le Bec Rouge; and Hameau le Borsat, Val Claret (near Club Med)

Coopérative Laitière de Haute Tarentaise Local retail branch of the Bourg-St-Maurice cooperative dairy, selling their own Beaufort cheese, butter and yogurt, as well as local honey, charcuterie and vins de Savoie. ⓐ Promenade de Tovière, Tignes-le-Lac

La Grange Great regional products shop stocking a wide range of vins de Savoie, liqueurs, oils and vinegars, preserves, honey, cheeses and traditional Savoyard kitchen implements. ⓐ Le Tichot building, place du Curling, Val Claret Centre

LANGUAGE
Phrasebook

PARLEZ-VOUS FRANÇAIS? DO YOU SPEAK FRENCH?

Having even a basic insight into the language of the country
you are visiting will help enormously in getting the maximum
enjoyment from your stay, allowing you to engage more readily
with your hosts and speeding up assistance when you need it.

Of course, French is the official language of the region, but
most of the tourism service personnel you will encounter will
speak and understand some English.

The following is a selection of useful words and phrases most
frequently needed on a snowsports holiday:

ENGLISH	FRENCH
Hello	Bonjour
Good morning	Bonjour
Good afternoon	Bon après-midi
Good evening	Bonsoir
Good night	Bon nuit
Goodbye	Au revoir
See you soon	À bientôt
Please	S'il vous plaît
Thank you	Merci
Yes	Oui
No	Non
How are you?	Comment allez-vous?
Very well thank you	Très bien merci
I don't understand	Je ne comprends pas
Sorry	Pardon
How much?	C'est combien?
Give me...	Donnez-moi...
Where is?	Où est?
Where are?	Où sont?
When?	Quand?
Why?	Pourquoi?
Open	Ouvert
Closed	Fermé

ENGLISH	FRENCH	ENGLISH	FRENCH
Monday	*Lundi*	Twelve	*Douze*
Tuesday	*Mardi*	Thirteen	*Treize*
Wednesday	*Mercredi*	Fourteen	*Quatorze*
Thursday	*Jeudi*	Fifteen	*Quinze*
Friday	*Vendredi*	Sixteen	*Seize*
Saturday	*Samedi*	Seventeen	*Dix-sept*
Sunday	*Dimanche*	Eighteen	*Dix-huit*
Winter	*L'hiver*	Nineteen	*Dix-neuf*
Summer	*L'été*	Twenty	*Vingt*
One	*Un*	Thirty	*Trente*
Two	*Deux*	Forty	*Quarante*
Three	*Trois*	Fifty	*Cinquante*
Four	*Quatre*	Sixty	*Soixante*
Five	*Cinq*	Seventy	*Soixante-dix*
Six	*Six*	Eighty	*Quatre-vingts*
Seven	*Sept*	Ninety	*Quatre-vingt-dix*
Eight	*Huit*	Hundred	*Cent*
Nine	*Neuf*	First	*Le premier*
Ten	*Dix*	Second	*Le deuxième*
Eleven	*Onze*	Third	*Le troisième*

ENGLISH	FRENCH

PHRASES

What time is it?	*Quelle heure est-il?*
I would like	*Je voudrais*
Do you speak English?	*Parlez-vous anglais?*
Could you show me?	*Pouvez-vous me l'indiquer?*
Could you help me?	*Pouvez-vous m'aider?*
Where are the toilets?	*Où sont les toilettes?*
I've lost...	*J'ai perdu...*

ACCIDENTS / SICKNESS / EMERGENCIES

I don't feel well	*Je ne me sens pas bien*
Doctor	*Médicin*
I've had a fall	*Je suis tombé*
I'm dizzy	*J'ai des vertiges*
It hurts here	*J'ai mal ici*
There's been an accident	*Il y a eu un accident*
Dentist	*Dentiste*

ENGLISH	FRENCH
ACCIDENTS / SICKNESS / EMERGENCIES	

I've got...	*Je souffre de...*
Constipation	*Constipation*
Diarrhoea	*Diarrhée*
Earache	*Mal d'oreille*
Headache	*Mal de tête*
Stomach ache	*Mal d'estomac*
Sunstroke	*Coup de soleil*
Ankle	*Cheville*
Arm	*Bras*
Ear	*Oreille*
Eye	*Oeil*
Hand	*Main*
Head	*Tête*
Foot	*Pied*
Leg	*Jambe*
Wrist	*Poignet*
Condom	*Préservatif*
Tampons	*Tampons*

DIRECTIONS AND PLACES

Left	*À gauche*
Right	*À droite*
Straight ahead	*Tout droit*
I've lost my way	*Je me suis égaré*
Phonebox	*Cabine téléphonique*
Post office	*La poste*
Post box	*Boîte aux lettres*
Postage stamp	*Timbre*
Supermarket	*Supermarché*
Tourist information	*Office de tourisme*

AT THE RESTAURANT

Do you have a menu in English?	*Vous avez la carte en anglais?*
The wine list	*Carte des vins*
Dish of the day	*Plat du jour*
The bill	*L'addition*
Bottle	*Bouteille*
Corkscrew	*Tire-bouchon*

ENGLISH	FRENCH
AT THE RESTAURANT	
Toothpick	*Cure-dent*
Wine glass	*Verre*
Tumbler	*Verre*
Beer	*Bière*
Draught beer	*Bière pression*
Red wine	*Vin rouge*
White wine	*Vin blanc*
Rosé	*Vin rosé*
Water	*Eau*
White coffee	*Café au lait*
Beef	*Boeuf*
Bread	*Pain*
Butter	*Beurre*
Cheese	*Fromage*
Chicken	*Poulet*
Dessert	*Déssert*
Egg	*Oeuf*
Fish	*Poisson*
Ice cream	*Glace*
Lamb	*Agneau*
Meat	*Viande*
Poultry	*Volaille*
Roast	*Rôti*
Salad	*Salade*
Soup	*Potage*
Vegetables	*Légumes*
SKI TERMS	
I'd like a ski pass	*Je voudrais un forfait de ski*
To rent	*Louer*
To ice skate/ice skates	*Patiner/Patins à glace*
Avalanche	*Avalanche*
Bindings	*Fixations*
Cable car	*Téléphérique*
Chair lift	*Télésiège*
Cross-country skiing	*Ski de fond*
Drag lift	*Téléski*
Goggles	*Lunettes de ski*
Gloves	*Gants*

ENGLISH	FRENCH
SKI TERMS	
Gondola	*Télécabine*
Mountain	*Montagne*
Passport photo	*Photo d'identité*
Ski boots	*Chaussures de ski*
Ski poles	*Bâtons de ski*
Skis	*Skis*
Ski wax	*Fart à ski*
Snowchains	*Chaînes de neige*
Socks	*Chaussettes*
Suncream	*Crème solaire*
Ski lessons	*Leçons de ski*

TEMP:	°C	−25	−20	−15	−10	−5	0	5	10	15	20	25	30
	°F	−13	−4	5	14	23	32	41	50	59	68	77	86

CONVERSIONS

DISTANCES

Centimetres to inches	x 0.394
Inches to centimetres	x 2.540
Yards to metres	x 0.914
Metres to yards	x 1.094
Miles to kilometres	x 1.609
Kilometres to miles	x 0.621

AREA

Acres to hectares	x 0.405
Hectares to acres	x 2.471

HEIGHT

Metres to feet	x 3.281
Feet to metres	x 0.305

ACCURACY

Conversion formulas are rounded up to 3 decimal places, therefore, calculations may result in slight differences in practice.

HEALTH & SAFETY
Piste security

PREPARATION FOR SNOWSPORTS

It's all too easy in these times of low-cost travel and rapid communications to forget that you're travelling from a relatively benign temperate climate straight into Arctic conditions. Furthermore, you're going to be careering around this wild and inhospitable environment standing on two planks or a tray, moving at the speed of a car with not much more than a knitted beanie and a pair of padded gloves to protect you! The only way to ensure your safety and get maximum enjoyment out of your trip is to have respect for the seriousness of the situation you're putting yourself in and prepare accordingly.

Preparation begins at home: join a gym, ride a bike or just walk further and more often. The best and safest skiers and snowboarders are fit ones.

Once in your resort, warm-up at the start of each day and after rest breaks. A few minutes' stretching and/or jogging on the spot will pay dividends in your ability to sustain activity and avoid injury.

Weather conditions in the high mountains change rapidly and dramatically, so dress for all eventualities – it's easier to cool down than it is to warm up. Most heat loss occurs through your head, so always wear a hat. In the tricks parks and when freeriding, wear a helmet – all the best riders do.

ESSENTIAL ITEMS

Carry the following items with you on the mountain:

- water
- sunblock for skin and lips
- a piste map
- spare clothing
- high-energy snacks
- basic first-aid kit

PROTECTING YOURSELF FROM THE EFFECTS OF ALTITUDE

Temperature is inversely proportional to altitude: the higher you go, the lower the temperature drops.

Every 100 m (328 ft) rise in altitude above sea level equates to a shift north of around 161 km (100 miles). By the time you get up to 2500 m (8203 ft) that's equivalent to going from London to the Arctic Circle.

Conversely, the sun's radiation increases with altitude. For every 100 metres you go up, solar UV intensifies by about 2 per cent; so at 2500 metres you're being fried twice as quickly as you would be on a Mediterranean beach.

On overcast and snowy days, the clouds only disperse the UV-rays but don't stop them. Sunscreens absorb a set percentage of the UV reaching you; only a total sunblock and technical eyewear will provide maximum protection. Don't forget that snow reflects the sunlight and UV-rays – make sure you protect under your chin, below and behind your ears, under your nose and your eyelids. Goggles provide all-round protection and enhanced visibility; sunglasses are fine for wearing on the terraces or strolling around a resort, but they're not for riding in. Wearing a hat not only keeps you warm, but protects you from sunstroke too.

Dehydration is a problem in all active sports. When you add an increase in altitude to the equation, the problem becomes compounded and potentially fatal. Dehydration leads to fatigue, and tiredness is the primary cause of most accidents, injury and hypothermia. The best way to ensure that you're well hydrated is to start that way and maintain a good fluid balance throughout the day. The trick is to sip water or isotonic fluids little and often. Invest in a hydration backpack or carry a couple of bottles of water with you.

GEAR SAFETY

Ski boots weren't designed for walking on the piste. On steep slopes it's always safer to keep your skis or snowboard on. If you take them off and there's ice underfoot you'll have even less control than you had with your gear on.

When you do take your gear off, make sure that it is secured. If your skis or board slide away they can severely injure or kill someone in just the few seconds it takes them to pick up velocity. Legally you are responsible: this is not an accident but an avoidable lack of care.

Put your gear in a rack if there is one available. If not, make sure you set your board down upside-down so that your bindings dig into the snow. Skis should be set down with their brake legs digging into the snow or placed upright and rammed deep into the snow where they can't run away if they fall over. Don't lean gear on the sides of cable car cabins or on flat walls. It will slide off and knock down others and they're just like a guillotine when they come crashing down.

AU DELÀ DE CE PANNEAU VOUS ENTREZ DANS
UN DOMAINE HORS PISTE À VOS RISQUES ET PÉRILS
NI BALISE - NI SÉCURITÉ - NI PATROUILLE

THIS IS WHERE THE SKI SLOPES END
CONTINUE AT YOUR OWN RISK
NO MARKERS - NO BARRIERS - NO PATROLS

AN DIESEM SCHILD ENDEN DIE PISTEN
WEITERFAHRT AUF EIGENE GEFAHR
KEINE MARKIERUNGEN - KEINE ABSICHERUNG - KEINE PATROUILLEN

AVALANCHE RISK WARNINGS

Plain yellow flag = risk levels 1 to 2:
low to moderate probability of avalanche

Chequered yellow and black flag = risk levels 3 to 4:
moderate to high probability of avalanche

Black flag = risk level 5:
absolute risk of large avalanche

ⓘ Zero risk does not exist! Always be aware and prepared.

OFF-PISTE

ⓘ Check if your insurance policy covers off-piste skiing then follow these rules for optimum safety:

● Never leave the marked ski area on your own, it's safest to travel in groups of three persons minimum.

● Unless you know the area like the back of your hand, always employ a qualified mountain guide.

● Never blindly follow someone else's tracks, they may lead in the wrong direction or even off a cliff!

● Always carry the essential off-piste kit: avalanche transceiver, shovel, probe, map and compass.

If travelling off-piste in glacial areas you should also carry a climbing rope, harness, ice screws, carabiners and rope ascenders/foot slings. However, these items are only effective if you know what they are for and how to use them properly. Many resorts run avalanche awareness and safety equipment training courses. The golden rule is: get wise or get lost!

◀ *Piste signs and markers have been put there by mountain professionals – respect them! They are there not just to protect you, but to protect others too*

SLOPE RULES & REGULATIONS

The International Ski Federation (FIS) has set rules for slope users. These have established a legal precedent. Failure to abide by these rules may result in your ski pass being annulled and you may be banned from using the installations and the slopes. If you cause injury or death you may also be charged with negligence or manslaughter. The following is a summary:

1. Slope users must not endanger others.
2. You must adapt speed and behaviour to your ability and to current conditions.
3. The slope user in front always has priority.
4. When overtaking, leave room for those in front to manoeuvre.
5. Check uphill and downhill before you enter, start or cross pistes.
6. Only stop at the sides of the piste. If you have fallen, clear the slope quickly.
7. When moving up or down on foot, keep to the side of the piste.
8. Respect all piste signs and station information.
9. In the case of accidents, always give assistance.
10. You must give your identity to the Piste Patrol, Emergency Services and other accident victims when requested.

INSURANCE

Accident insurance is not included in ski pass prices. Make sure you are adequately covered or take the insurance supplement. Never travel without comprehensive winter sports travel insurance and always ensure that you are covered for on-mountain rescue and transport to hospital, on top of medical treatment and hospitalization cover. Some sports, such as paragliding and snowmobiling, are not covered by standard travel insurance and you will need to take out extra cover for these.

INTRODUCTION

Welcome to one of France's longest established ski resorts and one of the most respected and prestigious wintersports destinations in the world.

Ever since the first ski lift was installed in 1934, Val d'Isère has remained in the snowsports spotlight and has developed an enviable pedigree. It is home to the prestigious Critérium de la Première Neige race, which launches the Alpine Ski World Cup season every year, and host to more than 150 World Cup competitions, plus the blue riband events of the 1992 Albertville Winter Olympics. It is also a member of the exclusive club of the world's top ski resorts, achieving the Alpine grand slam thanks to its successful bid to host the 2009 World Alpine Ski Championships.

One of the primary reasons for Val d'Isère's successful bid for the world championships was the innovative marketing of the town's unique ability to stage a face-to-face event. The men's courses will be on the existing Olympic 'Face du Bellevarde', with the women's courses directly opposite on the Solaise; the two finish areas are within 50 m (55 yd) of each another. Athletes, spectators and the press will all be able to simply stroll into the grandstand areas in the middle of the town's base slopes, and the championships are being hailed as the first to be 'car free'.

PRONUNCIATION

Val d'Isère	val~dis~air	**La Daille**	la~dye
Le Fornet	lu~forn~eh	**Le Laisinant**	lu~lay~sin~on

◀ *The attractive heart of Val d'Isère's old village*

The town itself has not been overshadowed by the focus on the surrounding ski area. The attractive tranquil core of the original village remains and in 1998 a project was initiated to renovate and landscape the more modern resort centre, with priority for pedestrians, more trees and shrubs and an emphasis on more traditionally styled architecture. The mission continues and the effects are laudable. The resulting ambiance is worlds apart from some of France's purpose-built ski stations.

Although retaining its authentic Savoyard soul, the town also enjoys a phenomenal partisan following in the UK/Eire ski market, resulting in an almost 50/50 mix of French- and English-speaking visitors thronging its streets and slopes every winter, and fuelling a cosmopolitan and vibrant après-ski scene.

The area's main attraction, however, is still the quality and quantity of its skiing. Committed enthusiasts rank Val d'Isère beside Chamonix and La Grave as a full-on, serious snowsports station. The sheer extent and seriousness of the off-piste potential is a big draw, with wild high-altitude glacial zones and deep powder chutes that seem to go on forever, aided by a favourable microclimate that has delivered an average 6 m (20 ft) of the white gold every year. The resort primarily appeals to, and is ideally suited to, good intermediates and advanced riders, but the huge choice and variety of the accessible terrain means that there is something here for everyone.

The beginners' area is limited, but the high-altitude snowbowl beyond the summit of the Solaise offers a wonderful playground for progressing learners and early intermediates. The home runs to town are all red or black and are a bit too tricky for novices, but you can always descend using one of the numerous two-way lifts serving the base area (check the times for the last lift down).

The individual sectors that make up the local ski area are varied and give a different character to each day's skiing.

Pissaillas Glacier at the furthest, highest edge of the marked, but breachable, boundary is as high and wild as it sounds, but is accessible to most competent abilities, with good cruising blues flowing down the Iseran Valley towards **Le Signal** above **Le Fornet**.

The **Solaise sector** is Val's original core ski zone, with snow-sure, motorway-wide blue pistes groomed to perfection and undulating through a high, open snowbowl, finally swooping to the foot of the town on more challenging runs through sheltered wooded slopes.

The **Bellevarde sector** shares a high open snowbowl with **La Daille** sector, but possesses the jewel in the Espace Killy's on-piste crown, the long and steep Face black run, which challenged the world's best Alpine sports athletes at the 1992 Winter Olympics.

La Daille is also not short on pedigree. Its long OK red piste is the route for the Critérium de la Première Neige. This sector also links with Tignes to complete the Espace Killy domain.

A Mecca for experts and off-piste extreme ski enthusiasts, yet a popular family resort with high-quality accommodation and well-established services. Val d'Isère has consolidated its position as a serious snowsports station and remains a world-class all-rounder.

FURTHER INFORMATION
- Val d'Isère's tourist office: current information and an excellent resort guide, www.valdisere.com
- Val d'Isère radio 96.1FM: regular on-site weather, snow and piste grooming reports in English

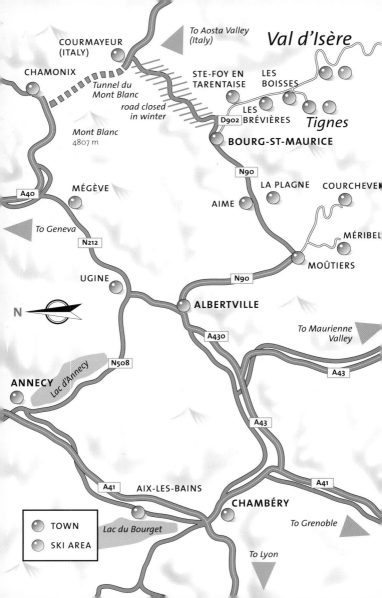

COMING & GOING

During the winter months, Val d'Isère is almost the last road-accessible point at the top end of the Tarentaise Valley (Le Fornet hamlet is the highest reachable point). The only route to the resort is the D902 road from Bourg-St-Maurice (31 km/19 miles). Bourg-St-Maurice can be reached by train (Eurostar, TGV or Thalys) or on the N90 road from Albertville (53 km/33 miles) via Moûtiers and Aime. Daily coach transfers are available from Bourg-St-Maurice and regularly from most of the international airports. Ⓦwww.altibus.com/ www.autocars-martin.com Of course, you could always fly straight in to the town's heliport at Le Crêt. Ⓦ www.saf-helico.com

By road: from Bourg-St-Maurice, the D902 passes through the village of Ste-Foy en Tarentaise and continues up the valley via a number of small tunnels to the first major junction point, the D87 turn-off for Tignes across the top of the impressive dam at the Lac du Chevril. Continue straight on for Val d'Isère on the D902. The road skirts the Lac du Chevril reservoir, with views up towards Tignes le Lavachet above right, winding through a series of dark and relatively narrow tunnels (caution for black ice caused by meltwater dripping inside the tunnels) to arrive at La Daille. Continue up the now straight main road past the next round-about (the 'Funival' funicular is over to the far right and the open parking here is free of charge for cars) towards Val d'Isère, which is just ahead through the suburb of Le Crêt.

At the first of the town's roundabouts, take the second exit to the right up rue Pigalle for the central covered car park, or continue straight up the main street for all other routes. At the next central roundabout, turn second right into the tunnel for Le Joseray, La Legettaz and Le Châtelard, or go straight on for Le Laisinant and Le Fornet.

VAL D'ISÈRE TOWN PLAN

KEY

i	Information office	🚡	Ski pass sales point
🚠	Cable car	✂	Equipment hire shop
🚏	Bus stop	P	Parking
€	ATM cash machine	🏪	Supermarket
+	Medical centre	+	Pharmacy
✉	Post office	†	Church

HOTELS & APARTMENTS

❶ Hotel Morris
❷ Hotel Brussels
❸ Hotel Grand Paradis
❹ Hotel Mercure

❺ Hotel Tsanteleina
❻ Hotel Blizzard
❼ Hotel Christiania
❽ Hotel Barmes de l'Ours

RESTAURANTS (see pages 169–70)

❶ La Grande Ourse
❷ La Casa Scara
❸ Maison Chevallot

❹ Les 3 Bises
❺ Bar Jacques
❻ La Casserole

BARS & CLUBS (see pages 171–2)

❶ Pacific
❷ Bar l'Alexandre
❸ Saloon
❹ Warm Up Café

❺ Bananas
❻ Dick's 'T' Bar
❼ Le Petit Danois
❽ La Forêt

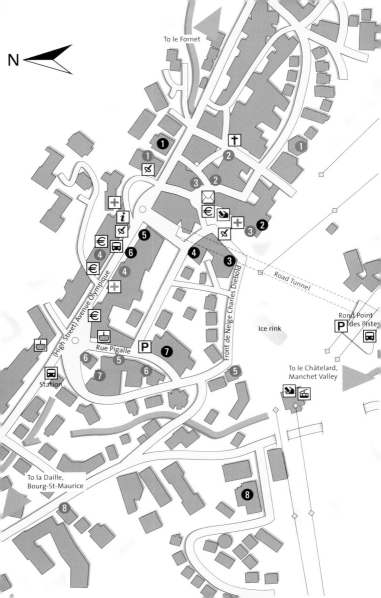

SKI AREA DATA

- Opening time   08.45 hours
- Last lift up   17.00 hours
- Skiable area   1200 ha (2965 acres)
- Altitude   1550 to 3456 m (5086 to 11,339 ft)
- Vertical drop   906 m (2973 ft)
- Access points   7
- Ski schools   20 +

• Ski lifts	90		
Funiculars	2	*Non-declutchable chair lifts*	25
Cable cars	4	*Declutchable chair lifts*	19
Gondolas	4	*Rope tows*	6
Drag lifts	30	*Free lifts*	10
• Capacity	155,925 passengers/hour		

• Pistes	131 (= 300 km/186 miles)		
Green	20	*Tricks parks*	2
Blue	60	*Halfpipes*	3
Red	35	*Children's*	4
Black	16	*Nordic*	44 km (27 miles)

- Hands-free ski pass   No
- Snowmaking   331 cannons
- First-aid posts   9
- Medical centres   5
- Mountain bars/restaurants   17 sites
- Visitor information   www.valdisere.com

Figures given are for the full Espace Killy domain

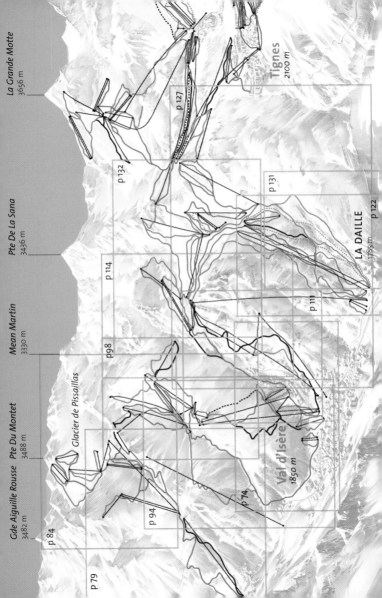

La Grande Motte
3656 m

Tignes
2100 m

p 127

p 132

p 131

Pte De La Sana
3436 m

LA DAILLE
1785 m

p 122

p 114

Mean Martin
3330 m

p 98

p 111

Pte Du Montet
3488 m

Gde Aiguille Rousse
3482 m

Glacier de Pissaillas

Val d'Isère
1850 m

p 74

p 94

p 84

p 79

SKI PASSES

All the options available are full Espace Killy passes covering
Val d'Isère and Tignes (only when the links are open). Prices are
consistent throughout the season, with no high season supplements. A photograph is required for all ski passes of more than
one day's duration. The passes are not electronically readable
and must be displayed at all times. Lost passes will not be
replaced or refunded.

All passes are available for children (5–12 years), adults (13–59
years) and seniors (60–74 years): half-day – on sale from 12.30
hours (13.00 in spring); full-day and multiples thereof up to 21
days – the longer the duration, the cheaper the equivalent daily
rate; full season – covering the entire season for the whole Espace
Killy domain.

Ski passes are free of charge for all children under 5; for 5–12
year olds prices are about 25 per cent cheaper than those of adults.
Ski passes for guests aged 60–74 are about 15 per cent cheaper
than standard adult passes; passes are free for the over 75s.

Bad-weather insurance is automatically included for all ski
passes of between 3 and 21 days' duration. If bad weather closes
all the lifts, then your ski pass will be reimbursed for all the days
you were unable to ski except for one grace day.

❶ Proof of age is required at the time of purchase for all child
and senior ski passes.

SWAP RESORTS

Espace Killy ski passes of minimum six days' duration permit
a free-of-charge day-pass for Paradiski (Les Arcs & La Plagne),
Trois Vallées (Courchevel, Meribel, Les Menuires, Val Thorens) and
Valmorel; plus, reduced-price day-passes at La Rosière and Ste-Foy.

SKI PASS SALES POINTS

You can purchase any of the passes offered at any of the sales booths that are dotted around the resort and base stations (see town plan on page 59). The main sales points are:

Le Fornet At the cable car base station.

La Daille Beside the Funival funicular base station.

Val d'Isère At the town centre ski pass office near the post office, and at the Solaise area piste-side kiosks at l'Olympique cable car station/Sun Bar building. Photo booths are available at the town centre ski pass office and the Sun Bar building.

If you can present your old ski pass from any of the previous three seasons, you will receive a discount of at least three per cent on a new one at the time of purchase.

NON-SKIERS

Non-skiers wishing to travel up to the high-altitude restaurants and viewpoints can purchase a 'pedestrian pass' permitting one round trip on any of the eight ski lifts that are accessible to pedestrians: these are Le Fornet cable car, Vallon de l'Iseran gondola, Solaise cable car, l'Olympique cable car, Bellevarde Express chair lift, Loyes Express chair lift, Funival funicular and Daille gondola.

🛈 Accident insurance is not included in ski pass prices. Make sure you are adequately covered (see page 50).

PRICES
For current prices of ski passes and other resort services, go to our website: **www.ski-ride.com**

FREE LIFTS

There are a number of beginners' zones lifts in both Val d'Isère and La Daille that are free of charge and open to all responsible adults, so do not require a ski pass to use. These are the Lanches ski tows at La Daille; and the Savonnette and Legettaz ski tows and the Village and Rogoney chair lifts at Val d'Isère town slopes.

SKI BUS

Three lines are operated by the ski-bus service:

➔ **Red Line**   Le Fornet ≫ Le Laisinant ≫
(Train Rouge)   Val d'Isère centre/Rond Point des Pistes ≫
                   Funival ≫ La Daille

➔ **Blue Line**   Rond Point des Pistes ≫ Club Med ≫
(Train Bleu)   Legettaz

➔ **Green Line**   Rond Point des Pistes ≫ Joseray ≫
(Train Vert)   Châtelard ≫ Manchet

The Green and Blue Lines run from 07.00 on Saturdays, 10.00 on weekdays, and continue until 20.00 at roughly 15-minute intervals. The Red Line begins at 08.30 and continues until just after 02.00 the next morning. Between 08.30 and 17.30 the service is non-stop, approximately every 5 minutes; from 17.30 to 20.00 it runs every 10 minutes and after 20.00 about every half hour. The bus stop at the Funival in La Daille is a get-off-only stop between 08.30 and 16.00.

Timetables are posted on the bus stops and are available from the tourist board and most hotels. Note that there is a reduced service at the beginning and end of the season. The service is free of charge for all visitors – no ski pass is required.

EQUIPMENT

Most visitors travelling with a tour operator tend to leave the organization of equipment to their reps. New arrivals are usually taken en masse for gear fitting on their first morning. Virtually every sports shop in Val d'Isère town has a snowsports equipment rental operation. All of the major franchises are represented, among them Sport2000 and Twinner, InterSport and SkiSet, and there are a number of excellent independent shops offering bespoke services.

Since Val d'Isère attracts such a high percentage of advanced and regular snowsports enthusiasts, equipment hire quality, customer service and attention to detail tend to be very high. This is nowhere more evident than at Precision, a technical sales and rental business consistently voted the best ski-hire shop in the Alps. They have built their reputation on offering the highest level of technical advice and, as founders of the Snowtec brand guarantee for technical excellence, have set the benchmark for specialist snowsports shops, designing and delivering world-class training programmes to other snowsports businesses throughout Europe.

Precision's 'Pacific' shop, located in a prime position opposite the tourist office in Val d'Isère town centre, is the nerve centre of the operation, housing a large technical equipment and clothing shop, plus a very slick equipment rental operation. The business caters for all levels of ability, but focuses squarely on advanced and off-piste riders, with a wide range of back-country safety equipment and technical kit on offer. It also operates one of the world's most advanced boot-fitting centres (in the square beside Val d'Isère's post office), as well as its own Snowtec test centre at La Daille, where clients looking to purchase skis or boards can try the whole gamut of latest models before they buy.

Ⓦ www.precision-ski.com

TUITION

As befits a ski station of this extent and international renown, there is no shortage of choice when it comes to ski schools and courses available. There is everything from standard group lessons for absolute beginners and progressing novices, up to advanced one-to-one teaching clinics for expert all-mountain riders. As well as the big two national ski school operations, ESF and Snow Fun, there are a number of specialized independent ski schools. The following are some of the best:

Evolution 2: ski and outdoor adventure tuition. Ski, snowboard, off-piste, Telemark, Nordic, heliskiing, plus adventure activities such as ice diving, paragliding and Arctic dogsled mushing.
Ⓦ www.evolution2.com

The Development Centre: small professional team of highly qualified British coaches offering group clinics (maximum class size, six) and private development sessions; tailored for all abilities.
Ⓦ www.tdcski.com

Mountain Masters: highly qualified small team of British and French ski instructors and mountain guides offering private and group lessons (maximum class size, six) with video feedback; private coaching and off-piste guiding.
Ⓦ www.mountain-masters.com

Misty Fly: specialist snowboard school offering courses for all levels; also off-piste and freestyle. Snow and avalanche briefings given at the start of every week.
Ⓣ +33 (0)4 79 40 08 74

CHILDCARE

Since most childcare services in resort include outdoor activities, please ensure that your children are prepared with warm clothing, gloves, proper sunglasses or goggles, handkerchiefs and sun protection lotion. Helmets are also strongly recommended.

The ESF (École du Ski Français): operate gentle Snow Gardens fenced off at the foot of the town slopes in both Val d'Isère and La Daille. The zones are equipped with magic carpet conveyors or rope tows, colourful obstacles and cartoon character statues, and specialist nursery ski instructors introduce children aged 4–5 years to the world of snowsports. The service is bookable for either 2 or 3 hours in the mornings and for 2½ hrs in the afternoons. Ski hire is not included. Ⓦ www.ski-ecole.com

Le Village des Enfants: the Village is a dedicated crèche located at the base of the Solaise sector slopes, just above the Rond Point des Pistes square and bus stops. It is bookable for a half day, full day or week, and meals are optional. Children are supervised by a team of qualified nursery instructors and take part in a variety of indoor and outdoor leisure and learning activities. They can also take skiing lessons. Equipment hire is not included. Ⓣ +33 (0)4 79 40 09 81

Le Petit Poucet: transport to and from accommodation, and to and from ski lessons is provided for free for attending children throughout the day. Indoor and outdoor activities, computer games and ski and snowboard rental coordination are provided. The services are available by the hour, half day or full day, for children aged 3 years plus. Ⓦ www.garderielepetitpoucet.com

SERVICES

Medical centres: there are well-equipped trauma and X-ray suites available at three separate medical centres in Val d'Isère: two in the town centre plus the larger MédiVal centre on the main road near Le Crêt. All are quickly accessible from the foot of the Solaise slopes and from the other sectors. The MédiVal site also houses a large pharmacy and physiotherapy suite. Val d'Isère, along with Tignes, has a network of on-piste first-aid posts dotted around the mid- and high-level ski area. All first-aid posts are permanently staffed by the piste patrol.

Cabinet Médical du Val Village	☎ +33 (0)4 79 06 13 70
Cabinet Médical du Centre	☎ +33 (0)4 79 06 06 11
Centre Médical MédiVal	☎ +33 (0)4 79 40 26 80

In cases of injury or illness, the medical staff will contact your insurance company, although you will have to pay any initial costs, excluded by any excess clauses, on site. Make sure that your insurance covers heli-rescue, piste rescue and ambulance transport, as well as medical and hospital expenses.

❶ Always have on you some form of identification and your insurance details. It is also advisable to carry a small first-aid kit with you for dealing with minor cuts and bruises (see Health & Safety, pages 46–50).

Telephones: phonecard and coin-operated public telephone booths are plentiful within the town itself, and once out on the slopes there are public telephones sited at all the largest mountain restaurants.

GSM mobile phone coverage is virtually 100 per cent.

WCs: located at the base stations of the Daille gondola, the Olympique and Solaise cable cars, and the upper Funival station. All mountain restaurants also have public toilets; many are serviced and levy a small charge.

ATMs: cash machines are dotted around Val d'Isère town. The closest to the slopes is at the post office, which can be reached via the pisted square extending towards the town centre between the Hotel Brussels and the Hotel Grand Paradis.

Mountain restaurants: there are a dozen different sites in the Val d'Isère ski area, which are directly accessible by piste. All offer a full bar service and most have snack food and self-service fare in canteen-style surroundings. Around half also have good à la carte restaurants, offering more refined gastronomic menus and ambiance; reservations are required at busy periods.

There is also a choice of further good restaurants and cafés at both La Daille and Val d'Isère base areas, again easily accessible direct from the pistes.

➜ *See page 147 for specific reviews.*

Picnic areas: the only official facility is provided on the Tête de Solaise restaurant terrace. There is a designated picnic area set out with some tables and chairs on the snow behind the snack kiosks serving the terrace. It is a pleasant enough spot and effectively shares the bustle and buzz of the main terrace. It is forbidden to picnic on any of the restaurant terraces. Otherwise, anywhere safe on the mountain is fine. To protect this beautiful environment, please deposit all your rubbish, plus any that you find in a bin.

SNOWFALL HISTORY & ANALYSIS

Although precipitation is unpredictable at very long range, patterns do emerge that are observable over a number of seasons. Using this data, you can tell if your preferred period of travel has historically seen good snow cover. The magic figure is 100 cm (39 in) – once snow depth exceeds this mark, conditions are generally good throughout the ski area and will remain so for a more extended period.

Snowcover during Christmas and New Year has generally secured the launch straight in to the high season, with the February school holiday period also having good cover. Mid to late March is a good bet for late, or return, visits. Late spring snowfalls are fairly regular, often giving the season's best conditions.

The occasional disparity between the trends of the upper and lower slopes indicates that precipitation fell as snow on upper slopes and rain on lower slopes.

The chart below details combined averages recorded over three seasons immediately prior to the publication of this guide. Visit **www.ski-ride.com** for live snow reports.

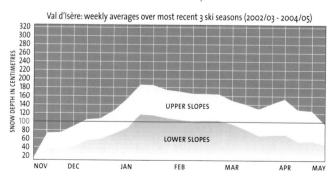

Val d'Isère: weekly averages over most recent 3 ski seasons (2002/03 - 2004/05)

PREVIOUS SEASONS' SNOWFALL BREAKDOWN BY YEAR

The following charts detail the snowfall history for the three most
recent seasons. Data from these charts was used to compile the
combined averages chart on the preceding page.

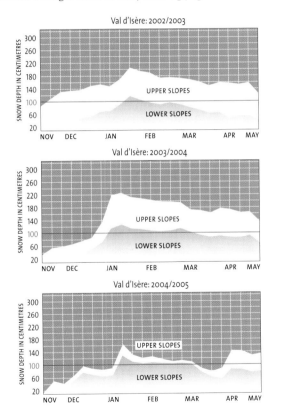

VAL D'ISÈRE BASE

When you first arrive at Val d'Isère's 'village' slopes, you really begin to see the attraction of the resort and a major reason for its success as an efficient snowsports station. The Front de Neige area of hotels and restaurants faces directly on to the foot of the slopes. The cable cars and chair lifts providing the prime access to the Bellevarde and Solaise sectors are clustered within walking distance, and the whole area is buzzing and attractive.

This village base area is the main focus for visitors of all abilities: as a departure point for keen intermediate and advanced skiers taking the main lifts to range out into this huge domain; for beginners and nervous novices in ski school classes on the gentlest wide lower slopes; for children discovering the joy of snowsports in the dedicated kiddies Snow Garden; for weekend dabblers availing themselves of the zone's free-of-charge ski lifts or skating on the attractive ice rink; and for non-skiers and locals for simply relaxing, sipping an aperitif, sunbathing and seeing and being seen.

The main approaches to the base area are either directly from the town centre, or from the Rond Point des Pistes area on the far side of the road tunnel from town. From the centre of town, simply stroll out on to the base area slopes, although you will need to walk across to the Rond Point des Pistes area to reach the Solaise cable car. From the main ski bus stop at the Rond Point des Pistes, the village slopes and lifts are accessible directly from the rear of the square by walking out on to the pistes. For the Solaise cable car, walk in the opposite direction slightly further up the road away from the road tunnel. All principal pistes from the Solaise and Bellevarde sectors return to this base area.

◐ Towards the Front de Neige, Val d'Isère

BEGINNERS' ZONE

The debutants' area here at the village base shares the slopes with the lowest sections of the main runs returning from the Solaise sector. The pistes can get very busy but the position, so close to the town and services, is ideal. The beginners' lifts are all free and no ski pass is required. They are: the two parallel Savonnette button lifts, furthest to the left on the Solaise side; and the village chair lift, nearest to town, departing from beside the ice rink. The short Savonnette lifts serve the gentlest and quietest slopes, with wide green pistes running back down either side of these button lifts.

The village lift is a non-declutchable, four-person chair lift, which again has two wide green pistes running down parallel to the lift-line. It is, however, often commented that the top of this area is quite steep for absolute beginners, so this is one to work up to. Also bear in mind that the Combe Martin black piste from the Solaise sector emerges from the tree line on your left in the lift's arrival area, joining the green pistes at this point, so do be alert to inconsiderate piste traffic. Another free lift (the Rogoney) departs from the base area, just to the right of the Solaise Express

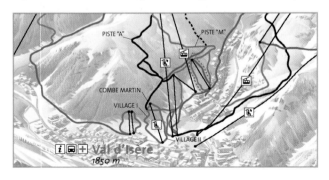

chair lift. It is named after, and follows the route of, the very first ski lift built in Val d'Isère, back in 1934. It travels over the Rond Point des Pistes square to provide uplift to the lowest Solaise sector slopes, and is useful for gaining height from the finish of the Face de Bellevarde to link with the Solaise cable car, and for accessing the Legettaz slalom course and the La Legettaz suburbs.

ROGONEY CHAIR LIFT

5 mins

- 164 m (538 ft) vertical rise
- 585 m (640 yd) long
- 2400 passengers/hour

On arrival, this is a reasonably flat area with routes away to the left and right: caution to the above left because the Piste "A" black route finishes by dropping in here. To the left, it is a short $3\frac{1}{4}$–$4\frac{1}{2}$ m (10–13 ft) skate to join the final section of the Combe Martin black piste under the line of the Solaise Express chair lift (steep and not suitable for beginners). Dismounting to the right takes you on to a fairly narrow but flat woodland track, heading in the direction of the Legettaz area. This track is manageable by confident beginners on their first forays out on the mountain, yet is still within sight of the town. The Legettaz button lift arrival point, and start of the Stade slalom course (red), is passed after around 150 m (164 yd). The track also continues ahead to merge with the home-run sections of the red Piste "M", by swinging down to the right and returning in the direction of town, passing the Solaise cable car base station on the way.

➔ For all other principal lifts and pistes in the Solaise sector, see page 91.

➔ For the Bellevarde sector, see page 109.

LE FORNET & PISSAILLAS SKI SECTOR

This is the highest sector in the Val d'Isère ski area and the most easterly limit of the domain, bordering on the wild and beautiful Vanoise National Park and close to the border with Italy.

It is split into three distinct zones: the short, wide blues and reds on the glacier; the long, cruising blues in the high Iseran Valley mid-section; and the steeper wooded slopes of the home runs back to the hamlet of Le Fornet.

Access is by cable car from Le Fornet, and via the Leissières Express chair lift or 3000 button lift from the Solaise sector. The Leissières Express chair lift also links in the opposite direction into the Solaise sector, to travel towards Le Laisinant and Val d'Isère.

FORNET CABLE CAR

3½ mins

- 383 m (1257 ft) vertical rise
- 1200 m (1312 yd) long
- 1000 passengers/hour

The base station is on the roadside beside the final stop of the Red Line ski bus. There is a large electronic piste map and information board on the façade, for informed route planning.

On arrival at the upper station, either remain in the building and go up the steps ahead to access the Vallon de l'Iseran gondola, for the onward journey towards the Pissaillas Glacier and upper slopes, or exit down the steps to the Signal restaurant. From here you can saunter over to the get-on points for the Signal and Pyramides button lifts, or go round to the left to the far side of the lifts station to start the Mangard blue and Forêt black pistes.

◀ *The open, cruising blues in the Iseran Valley*

MANGARD

This long, very good blue makes the home run to Le Fornet and has red characteristics. It starts as a narrow, steep and choppy access track from directly behind the lift station for the Fornet cable car and Vallon de l'Iseran gondola. The access track is shared with the start of the Forêt black run, which drops off almost immediately to the left after the initial entrance. The Mangard blue continues straight on as a narrow but gentle track before really starting by sweeping down to the left as a wide mild red profile slope – you can stay on the upper track to cut out this upper section. The road track rejoins from the right about 300 m (328 yd) below and the piste runs gently with it again before descending into the wooded slopes below. It is tempting to ride into the steeper and deeper glades to the sides, and there is a nice gully to ride in before dropping out to join the Cognan red piste below, but please respect this young plantation.

At its mid-section, the Mangard narrows and steepens to a fair red profile towards a piste junction point: go right and keep down the fall-line for the Cognan red, or swing left to remain on the Mangard. The Cognan is really just a variation of the Mangard and has a very similar profile, but with a laborious flat finish section.

The lovely Chalet Edelweiss restaurant is on the right-hand side of the Mangard piste a short way further on. Past the restaurant, the Mangard continues as a gentler route, which eventually runs out into a wide confluence finish area joined by the Forêt black from the left and the Cognon red from the right. All merge together and funnel across a little bridge for the last flat section towards the cable car station, so keep up momentum. The final few metres to the café and up the steps to the cable car/bus stop are a hike.

FORÊT

Begin from the rear of the lift station beside the Signal restaurant at 2330 m (7645 ft); the entrance track is shared with the Mangard blue, but is narrow and often choppy. The Forêt black then starts by dropping off to the left as a wide and frequently mogulled funnel heading into the tree line. The route swings left, but it is possible to go straight on into a steep off-piste gully to drop out on to the Mangard blue below. The Forêt itself narrows considerably and steepens to a good black, regularly with large moguls, for a very entertaining mid-section. The lower section of the run is a good fast red schuss into the convergence area with the Mangard/Cognon pistes and over the bridge to the cable car base station.

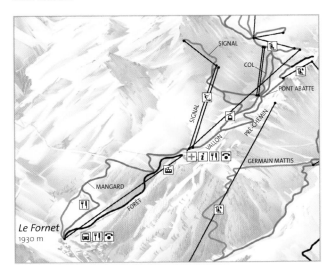

SIGNAL BUTTON LIFT

  8¼ mins
- Difficult lift; no novices
- 600 m (1969 ft) vertical rise
- 900 passengers/hour

❶ Avalanche risk information at get-on point.

Departing from just in front of the Signal restaurant terrace, to the left of the parallel Pyramides button lift, this steep button accesses the short but challenging Signal red piste, but is mostly used for access to l'Épaule du Petit Signal off-piste route. On the journey up, the lift takes a dogleg to the left to continue past the get-off point for the parallel Pyramides lift and to the steepest part of the ride. On arrival, dismount to the right to begin the Signal piste, or go straight ahead past the upper anchor pylon for the serious off-piste route – experts only!

❶ Note that snowboarders are not permitted to use the Pyramides button lift.

SIGNAL

The sole piste accessed by the Signal button lift and a good, albeit short, challenging red. The steep top section is frequently mogulled and can be a borderline black. The run remains consistent down to finish level with the Pyramides button lift get-off point. From here you can cross over the line of the Signal lift and continue as the Pyramide blue back to the base of these drags at the Signal restaurant and cable car/gondola station. The Pyramide piste is a standard wide blue. Another possibility is to ride off the upper section into the deeper stuff to the sides; the right-hand slope has rocky outcrops and cliff jumps, the left-hand side is more gentle and undulating, and just about allows you to link with the Col button lifts.

▲ *Towards Bellecôte from the top of the steep Signal red*

VALLON DE L'ISERAN GONDOLA LIFT

  12½ mins

- 452 m (1483 ft) vertical rise
- 2741 m (2998 yd) long
- 1500 passengers/hour

This is a slow old gondola departing from the Fornet cable car upper station. The external gear racks hold only skis; boards have to be taken inside. These gear holders are also a bit narrow and awkward for wide-tipped skis. Despite the rickety ride, the views towards Val d'Isère and La Daille and up to the towering peaks of La Tsanteleina and Le Dôme are terrific. On the upper portion of the journey, you also get a good view towards the Pissaillas Glacier.

On arrival, go straight out of the upper station and on to the flat area behind; the Cema chair lift linking from the glacier area arrives here to your left. There is a tool point and a piste map and information board here too.

Turn left to begin the Lac Cema green and Col/Pont Abatte blues. The Lac Cema green immediately turns right and runs parallel to the line of the Cema chair lift, as the flat and only link route towards the glacier.

PONT ABATTE

This is really just a link route, from the top of the Vallon de l'Iseran gondola and the Cema chair lift, towards the Leissières Express chair link, which goes up and over the arête into the Solaise sector. From the shared start at the Vallon/Cema lifts, the piste swings out to the left as a wide fast blue heading straight for the chair-lift get-on point. Keep right to access the chair lift, or bypass it and continue descending as a wide blue to merge with the Pré-chemin, Col and Vallon blues below.

COL/PRÉ-CHEMIN/VALLON

All of these wide cruising blues follow the route of the Col de l'Iseran road through this high, treeless valley running down to the Signal restaurant and the cable car/gondola station. If you have arrived from the gondola or the Cema chair lift, you start by simply taking the motorway-wide piste straight down the valley. Coming from the top of the Col drag lifts, the start is actually on the Lac Cema green piste and you are travelling against the flow of glacier-bound traffic before you get to this same point.

There are a number of variations out to the right and left: the right-hand side is the Col and the left-hand route is the Pont Abatte linking with Leissières Express lift. Following the Col blue, you come to a junction point after only 200 m (219 yd). Keep highest right for the Col or bear right to begin the Pré-chemin blue. All routes eventually converge near the get-on level for the twin Col drag lifts, splitting again in two to continue the descent. The left-hand route is the Pré-chemin, the right is the Col plus a linking variation of the Pyramide blue. The Pré-chemin gives the more interesting ride, narrowing through a wide gully that offers an opportunity to play off the sides. Both pistes merge again to pass a major Grand Randonée cairn and now combine to become the Vallon blue, with a further couple of variations around some higher ground ahead, for the final steeper section towards the restaurant and lifts station. At all stages of the descent there is plenty of opportunity to cross over the deeper inter-piste snow-fields for even more variation.

All these routes make a good link to the Signal restaurant and the Fornet cable car and Vallon de l'Iseran gondola. To continue descending on piste towards Le Fornet, go under the line of the gondola and round to the far side of the station building.

COL BUTTON LIFTS

| 4³/4 mins | • 223 m (732 ft) vertical rise
• 1230 m (1345 yd) long
• 900 passengers/hour x 2 |

Twin button drag lifts that serve the upper mid-section of the Iseran Valley, giving access to the top of all blue pistes descending the valley and gaining sufficient altitude to make the link over to the Cascade Express chair lift serving the Pissaillas Glacier.

On arrival, either U-turn to the right and join the flat Lac Cema green piste to get to the start of the Col, Pont Abatte and Pré-chemin blues, or go straight on for the short wide Lac Cema green (really blue) to a good link with the Cascade Express chair lift, which you can see directly ahead below. It is tempting to take a shortcut off the side to the right, but there is a little stream gully at the bottom that is a hassle to get out of and not worth the trouble.

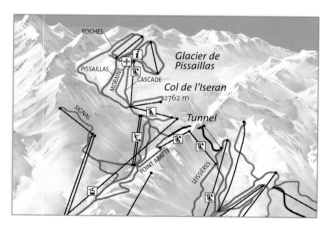

CASCADE EXPRESS CHAIR LIFT

- 415 m (1361 ft) vertical rise
- 1629 m (1781 yd) long
- 2200 passengers/hour

This is the prime lift providing uplift to the Pissaillas Glacier. The arrival area is flat and wide and gives great views over the entire glacier area and the peaks beyond; turn right to head to the Cote 3300 drag lift or to head off into the Pays Désert Glacier off-piste (experts only!). Alternatively, turn left for the Cascade and Moraine reds and to access the Pissaillas blue run and the Montets T-bar lift. There is a Ski Patrol/first-aid cabin just below, midway towards the Montets lift get-on point.

3300 T-BAR LIFT

- 205 m (673 ft) vertical rise
- 660 m (722 yd) long
- 1200 passengers/hour

T-bar rising to the highest lift-reachable point in the whole Val d'Isère ski area (3300 m/10,827 ft). The Montets T-bar lift runs parallel to the left and, despite how the piste map looks, arrives at a slightly lower altitude and serves more or less the same routes.

On arrival, turn right for the 3300 blue piste or to ride off beyond the boundary markers for the highest start for the Pays Désert off-piste glacier routes (experts only!). Alternatively, turn left for the Montets and Ouille pistes. The Montets T-bar lift is slightly lower over to your left and it is possible to ride over on the contour-line to its arrival point to access the Aiguille Pers blue and Roches red on the far side of the glacier along the base of the Aiguille Pers arête.

PISSAILLAS GLACIER

It is a great feeling to be so high in this wild sector, and to take in the far-reaching vistas over the Col de l'Iseran, the Réserve Naturelle de l'Iseran and towards Italy (ahead and right). This glacial area is the summer skiing area (*ski d'été*), open in July and August, and you can actually drive up and park near the upper station of the Vallon de l'Iseran gondola to access this high permafrost zone. Beyond the Col de l'Iseran watershed is the Maurienne Valley. The ski station of Bonneval-sur-Arc is the first village in that direction.

The main pistes on the glacier are quite short and all very similar in profile: the 3330 blue and green are basically twins running down parallel on each side of the 3330 T-bar; the Montets and Ouille blues are again almost twins, descending straight down the middle of the two lift-lines towards the base of the Montets lift. The Aiguille Pers blue descends on the far side of the Montets lift and is another wide, good blue beginning at the flat access traverse it shares with the Roches red.

🔺 *Towards the Pissaillas Glacier from Leissières Express*

OFF-PISTE ROUTES

Consult the information boards on arrival at the top of the Cascade Express chair lift or ask at the lift operator's hut for up-to-date information. For the Col Pers route, check too that the Gorges de Malpasset are passable before setting off.

❶ These routes are for experts only. Always employ a qualified local mountain guide whenever venturing off piste.

ROCHES

The longest piste on the glacier, beginning from the top of the Montets T-bar lift. Turn left on arrival from this lift to begin the flat traverse start. The Aiguille Pers blue also starts here after about 30 m (33 yd) by flowing off down to the left, parallel to the line of the arriving T-bar. The contour-line traverse at the top is green in character and brings the route as wide as possible out to the base of the cliffs at the Aiguille Pers arête, then sweeps down to begin the descent as a motorway-wide fast easy red. Keep high right to traverse to the Col for the classic Col Pers off-piste route.

The Combe du Géant red route joins from the left, coming from the base of the Montets T-bar lift as a continuation of the other upper pistes. After a further 200–250 m (219–273 yd), the Pissaillas blue joins sharply from the left. All continue as a standard wide blue towards the cluster of lifts ahead, with the Moraine red piste also dropping in to join from above left as you approach this confluence area. The nearest chair lift, on the left, is the Cascade Express. The chair lift ahead right is the Cema, which links with the upper station of the Vallon de l'Iseran gondola.

CASCADE & MORAINE

Twin fair reds that officially begin to the left on arrival at the top of the Cascade Express chair lift, although you can make either of these two pistes a continuation of your run from the top of the glacier to give a longer descent. Both are very similar in character – fast, well-groomed glacial pistes which take a reasonably entertaining fall-line parallel to the Cascade Express lift-line. The lower sections are the steepest and narrowest, dropping out on to the confluence area at the finish of the Roches piste and the cluster of lifts serving the glacier zone.

The Pissaillas blue piste is actually very similar and deserves its lesser grading only because it finishes less steeply by merging earlier with the flat final section of the Combe du Géant/ Roches red.

CEMA CHAIR LIFT

  4 mins

- 79 m (259 ft) vertical rise
- 491 m (537 yd) long
- 2200 passengers/hour

Since there is some higher ground separating the end of the glacier pistes from the top of the Iseran Valley blue pistes, the Cema chair lift exists to provide the short link out of the glacial zone for the return to the main sector. It arrives just facing the upper station of the Vallon de l'Iseran gondola, and you can take this, if you wish, down to the Fornet cable car station and Signal restaurant. Otherwise, turn right on arrival to begin the Col, Pont Abatte and Pré-chemin blues towards Le Fornet. The Pont Abatte route widest on the left links well with the Leissières Express lift to take you straight into the Solaise sector.

LEISSIÈRES EXPRESS CHAIR LIFT

4¹/₂ mins

- 1085 m (1187 yd) long
- 2400 passengers/hour

This is a fast link over the impressively rugged arête separating the Fornet and Solaise sectors, taking a vertigo-inducing up-and-over journey over the ridge.

The seriously steep, rutted route appearing out of the middle of the mountainside to the left on the first part of the journey is the Tunnel black route emerging from a tunnel through from the Solaise side, which is accessed using the 3000 button lift in the upper Solaise sector (see page 99).

On paper, the departure and arrival altitudes of this lift appear to provide a mere 31 m (102 ft) vertical rise, but you actually rise 277 m (909 ft) to clear the arête before dropping down into the Solaise sector, affording a stunning panorama over almost the entire Espace Killy domain.

On arrival, you are joining the Leissières and Plan Milet blues for onward routes.

● *Up and over on the Leissières Express*

SOLAISE SKI SECTOR

This is Val d'Isère's true home-sector ski domain, chiefly characterized by a wide, sunny snowbowl up on the higher reaches, enjoyable and manageable off-piste routes, the buzzing Tête de Solaise restaurant terrace and the testing home runs back to Val d'Isère town base.

Links can also be made towards the neighbouring high-altitude Pissaillas Glacier, Iseran Valley and Le Fornet sector. Almost the entire snowbowl, past the summit of the Solaise, is accessible by even early novices, being wide cruising blues. The prime access for the sector is via the Solaise cable car and Solaise Express chair lift directly from Val d'Isère base.

SOLAISE EXPRESS CHAIR LIFT

  7 mins

- 711 m (2333 ft) vertical rise
- 2028 m (2218 yd) long
- 2500 passengers/hour

This lift departs from the middle of the Val d'Isère base area and provides the largest volume uplift into the Solaise sector. The chairs are fitted with hoods, which can be lowered to shield you from rough weather. The journey up gives great views over the whole lower Solaise slopes and up the valley towards the Rocher du Charvet and Pointe de la Sana peaks.

On arrival, either turn right for the Tête de Solaise restaurant and to start all the home runs back to town, or go straight on via the flat track over the crest to head towards the rest of the sector and all links. There is a tool point by the fence on the left.

❶ Only three passengers are permitted per chair for descent.

◀ *Solaise cable car over the home run pistes*

SOLAISE CABLE CAR

- 671 m (2202 ft) vertical rise
- 1720 m (1881 yd) long
- 600 passengers/hour

The base station is a short distance from town, but an easy stroll from the Rond Pointe des Pistes and main ski-bus interchange. Steps lead up from the roadside to the edge of the final section of the Piste "M" run, which makes a good link from the lower Solaise sector slopes. A tool point for adjusting bindings is fixed to the wall by the entrance steps and there are WCs on the left just inside the building. The queue-line for the cable car is up the steps to the right. The ski pass desk sells pedestrian passes only.

On arrival at the upper station, exit to the right via the covered walkway around the rear of the building to emerge on the huge terrace at the Tête de Solaise restaurant. The Solaise chair lift arrives ahead left and the pistes begin at the far right-hand corner of the terrace. All of the home-run pistes – Piste "S" Naturide, Piste "A" black, Plan red, and the access to the Piste "M" red – start here on this open motorway-wide and totally pisted summit, running down under the line of the cable car. To continue towards the rest of the sector and head towards the link with Pissaillas/Le Fornet involves a short uphill hike to crest the summit. Instead, put your gear on and cruise over to the Terrasse button lift just below on the far side of this huge confluence area. This lift takes only two minutes and gains sufficient height to take you over the top of the Solaise. The chair lift arriving ahead left is the Lac. Keep to the right of this lift-line for the easy run down to the l'Ouillette bar/restaurant and the Madeleine chair lift, or go to the left, under the line of the chair lift, to ride towards the Glacier Express and Datcha lifts or the home-run routes to Le Laisinant.

ORIENTATION

The views from the summit of the Solaise are almost 360-degree and far reaching, giving you a great opportunity to get your bearings and orientate yourself within the Espace Killy domain. The best place to take in the views is at the arrival point of the Terrasse button lift, above the Tête de Solaise restaurant. Looking down the line of the arriving Lac chair lift, you are facing towards the Crête des Leissières arête separating the Solaise sector from the Fornet/Pissaillas sector. The wide snowbowl ahead on this side of the arête is a great novices' and early intermediates' playground, served by the Glacier Express, Cugnai, Datcha and Madeleine Express chair lifts. The valley to your left is the Super L area towards Le Laisinant.

Turning around, down the route of the Plan red and onward pistes past the Tête de Solaise restaurant, you are looking straight down the Isère Valley towards La Daille and the Lac du Chevril; sweeping left, the Rocher du Bellevarde with its famous Face black run, and the Bellevarde and upper La Daille sectors beyond.

Towards Crête des Leissières from the top of Solaise

PLAN / PISTE "M"

The whole summit of the Solaise is completely pisted and is a huge confluence zone for all routes passing this point to make the home runs to Val d'Isere; directional signage is poor but does exist. The upper section is a motorway-wide superpiste, manageable by the most competent novices, but lower level novices should take either the Solaise Express chair lift or Solaise cable car down to town.

The black Piste "S" Naturide leaves to the left after 400–450 m (440–495 yd); the Plan red continues to the right towards the tree line, keep following the Plan to access Pistes "M" and "A".

Ride over to the boundary ropes at the far right to access Le Lavancher and Les Danaïdes off-piste routes, or keep to the Plan and veer with the fall-line down to the left.

The next junction marks the end of the Plan piste: Piste "M" red peels off on the contour-line to the high left, Piste "A" black starts down to the right.

The "M" passes under the line of the Solaise Express chairlift to continue as a wider but often choppy piste cutting across the mountainside. Narrowing and swinging down to the right, it merges with the Legettaz area town slopes and passes the Solaise cable car base station on the final flat traverse towards Val d'Isère base and town.

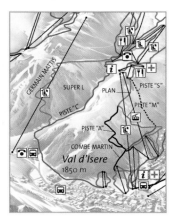

PISTE "A" / COMBE MARTIN

The Piste "A" will be the mid-section of the 2009 Alpine World Championships Women's course and remodelling will widen and alter its current route. From its mid-mountain start point, at the end of the Plan red, the "A" steepens and narrows though the trees, with a right-to-left camber and a good fall-line descent for its short but challenging and frequently choppy run.

At the junction below, you have the choice of leaving to the left to take a traverse track above the arrival point of the Rogoney chair lift towards La Legettaz and to link with the Solaise cable car, or you can keep to the right on the fall-line to begin the Combe Martin black.

The Combe Martin is a short but testing steep and frequently mogulled straight, heading directly for the central base area at Val d'Isère, with the church bell-tower and Hotel Brussels dead ahead; check your speed before entering the base area because you are merging with the beginners' zone.

PISTE "S"

This is a good knee-basher, taking the steepest fall-line descent off the Solaise towards Val d'Isère base. The "S" is the only Naturide route on this side of the Espace Killy, set aside as a protected and piste-mapped route, but left ungroomed for a more natural, deeper snow freeride experience. To reach it, take the upper Plan red and keep wide out to the left by the boundary fence: the "S" starts to the left by funnelling into a wide chute, which is usually mogulled from top to bottom and narrows as it reaches the tree line. The crux of the run is short but a good challenge, eventually dropping out to join the Piste "M" red towards Val d'Isère base and town.

PISTE "L"

This begins just above the first pylon of the Datcha chair lift, by branching off to the left down into the deep valley below. The entrance is fairly steep, but wide, with a mellow red profile. The route sweeps down to the right, at the base of some impressive cliffs and couloirs, to run as a wide standard blue along the valley floor heading straight for Le Laisinant. Approaching the village, you can turn sharp left to take the flat Traversée du Laisinant blue track all the way to Val d'Isère – it is an attractive woodland trail, but a real slog. For Le Laisinant, simply keep going straight on at the finish of the Piste "L", towards the village and for the Laisinant Express chair lift back up to the Solaise domain. (This chair lift is under construction and should be in place by the time you read this.)

GERMAIN MATTIS & SUPER L

Start just above the get-on level for the Datcha chair lift by taking the flat traverse track ahead right, remaining high on the contour-line above the Piste "L", which is far below left. The beautiful steep and deep off-piste shortcut down to the left is the Super L area, a great open freeride and an ideal first off-piste route – the later you leave the drop-in from the upper track, the longer the fun lasts!

The Germain Mattis also then begins by dropping off to the left: the top section is fair to good red, with a decent fall-line pitch. It is a short run but a fair one, its true value being the access it gives to the gorgeous Super L off-piste. The piste ends when it joins the Piste "L" blue on the valley floor.

▶ *Warning, or feature? Super L towards Tsanteleina*

GLACIER EXPRESS CHAIR LIFT

6 | 6¾ mins

- 322 m (1056 ft) vertical rise
- 1780 m (1947 yd) long
- 3000 passengers/hour

This is the main fast chair lift serving the wide Leissières snow-bowl. If linking from the Solaise, approach this lift by running under the lift-line to reach the get-on point, which is on the far side. The control gates operate on a staggered start basis, with each pair opening slightly before the others – watch the gates and not the passengers beside you for your cue to advance.

The journey up gives bird's-eye vistas over the entire snow-bowl, with the principal blues beneath you and the wide expanses of deep and steep off-piste lines on the whole wall of the Crête des Leissières up to your left. The chair lift going up and over the arête ahead left is the Leissières Express, linking towards the Pissaillas Glacier and the Fornet sector.

On arrival, dismount and veer left to start the wide Glacier, Plan Milet and Leissières Blues. The 3000 button lift and the Leissières Express chair lift are a short glide over to your right; keep highest to the right for the 3000 lift. The views are fantastic from here, giving you a truly commanding view over the whole domain.

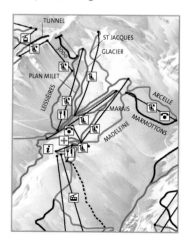

3000 BUTTON LIFT

2¹/₂ mins

- 173 m (568 ft) vertical rise
- 420 m (459 yd) long
- 600 passengers/hour

Note that snowboarders are not permitted to use this steep, difficult button lift, which serves the short 3000 black run and accesses the tunnel through to the upper Iseran Valley for the Tunnel black descent in the Pissaillas and Fornet sector. Just before you arrive at the top you can see the entrance to the tunnel immediately on your left. On arrival, leave sharply to the left on to the start of the very challenging 3000 black.

This lift is also great for providing uplift to reach the superb steep and deep freerideable walls of the Crête des Leissières arête.

3000

A short steep run on the wall of the Crête des Leissières, offering one of the Espace Killy's best on-piste challenges. The marked route begins immediately on arrival at the top of the 3000 button lift, accessed via the Glacier Express chair lift. The whole run is consistently steep and almost always heavily mogulled for the entire upper section. The views are worth pausing for, if you can lift your eyes from picking your line for a moment, with La Grande Motte above Tignes piercing the horizon ahead left. This slope also gives you the best opportunity to ride off to the left or right into the even more serious deep stuff on the side of the arête, as well as giving access to the entrance for the tunnel through the mountain to the Tunnel black run in the Pissaillas/Fornet sector. The tunnel mouth is only a few metres from the start, just to the left of the piste.

TUNNEL ●

This is a really exciting and tricky black, which is actually in the Fornet sector, but only accessible via a claustrophobic tunnel from the Solaise side. Take the steep 3000 button lift (snowboarders not permitted) and, after only 10–15 m (11–16 yd) on the very top section of the 3000 black piste, veer left to get to the tunnel mouth, usually partially obscured by snowdrifts; the entrance is locked if conditions are judged to be unsafe by the piste patrol.

Once you emerge on the other side, the ground drops away almost immediately and the route down is anyone's guess – just pick your line for short hop-turns down the steep, mogulled, rocky slopes. The Leissières Express chair lift back to the Solaise sector is at the bottom, or you can join the Pont Abatte blue onward into the Fornet/Pissaillas sector.

LEISSIÈRES EXPRESS CHAIR LIFT (TOWARDS PISSAILLAS) ○

- 1085 m (1187 yd) long
- 2400 passengers/hour

Fast link over the Crête des Leissières into the Fornet and Solaise sectors, taking a vertigo-inducing journey up-and-over the arête.

You rise 277 m (909 ft) to clear the arête before dropping down into the Fornet sector, providing a stunning panorama up to the Pissaillas Glacier ahead right and the whole upper Iseran Valley below left. On arrival, dismount to the right to join the Pont Abatte blue, U-turning to the right under the lift-line to head towards the Col button lifts for the quickest link to the glacier zone, or continue straight down the valley towards the Signal restaurant, Vallon de l'Iseran gondola and lower Fornet sector slopes.

◔ *Top of the 3000 black, towards La Grande Motte*

LEISSIERES/PLAN MILET/GLACIER

Sweeping motorway-wide blues ,which range over this wide snowbowl from the top of the Glacier Express chair lift, providing Val d'Isère's best playground for novices and early intermediates. The start area for all routes is to the left on arrival off the chair lift. It is also possible to hike around the lift anchor pylon to access the deeper undulating freeride over on that side.

All these pistes are variations on a similar theme: wide cruising through this open and sunny bowl, with plenty of opportunity to cross over between them to play in the deeper inter-piste snowfields. The Plan Milet takes the most direct route and therefore gives the most consistent run. All are manageable by competent novices. The views are great and the whole area has a wild, high-mountain atmosphere, yet is close to all major services.

The top section is a flat, shared area with the individual routes fanning out below. The Leissières route swings out wide to the right (passing the get-on point for the Leissières Express link lift towards Fornet/Pissaillas), curving along the base of the Crête des Leissières arête towards a good link with the Glacier Express chair lift again. The Glacier piste swings wide to the left under the line of the arriving chair to swoop over to the left-hand side of the snowbowl for the gentlest of the routes. The Plan Milet goes straight down the middle, parallel to the lift-line. The Plan Milet and the Glacier eventually converge and flow a little steeper for a good link to the Datcha restaurant and Cugnai chair lift. Bypassing these to the left takes you towards the l'Ouillette rope tow to link to the top of the Solaise towards Val d'Isère, or you can simply keep going to reach the Glacier Express and Datcha chair lifts. All three routes also allow you to keep descending into the valley below for Le Laisinant.

CUGNAI CHAIR LIFT

13 mins

- 390 m (1280 ft) vertical rise
- 2008 m (2196 yd) long
- 1000 passengers/hour

This is the longest and slowest of the four chair lifts serving this lovely high snowbowl, accessing a sole red piste (the St Jacques), but providing uplift to the famous Le Manchet Valley off-piste routes.

The direction of travel is directly south-east, with wide-reaching views over this whole upper area. On arrival, U-turn to the right and quickly clear the limited arrival area to begin the St Jacques, or go to the boundary rope ahead to access the Manchet drop-in. It is also possible to hike up to the summit of Cugnai, above right, for the most extreme start into the Manchet Valley. ❶ Note that the upper Manchet Valley off-piste slopes face south-east and are in full sun. Wind slabs also build on the highest slopes. This route is therefore best tackled before 13.00 hours, because the snow can be unstable later in the afternoon.

ST JACQUES

Accessed using the Cugnai chair lift. The views over the Manchet Valley towards the Rocher du Charvet, Pointe de la Sana and La Grande Motte are amazing and well worth the slow trip up.

The top section is a quite narrow fair-to-good red, swinging under the line of the arriving chair lift. There is plenty of opportunity to ride off to the left (best) and right into the steep and deep at the sides, before the piste itself mellows out into a plain fast schuss to merge with the Col de la Madeleine blue, flowing fast down towards the Datcha restaurant area and the Cugnai chair-lift base again.

DATCHA CHAIR LIFT

6³/4 mins

- 199 m (653 ft) vertical rise
- 845 m (924 yd) long
- 2365 passengers/hour

Queues frequently build up at this older fixed chair lift at busy periods. Approach from the right to join the queue-line for the control gates. There is a tool point at the get-on area.

A good use of this lift is to gain height from the lower bowl to take the Marais piste linking with the Lac chair lift towards Solaise, rather than slogging on the l'Ouillette rope tow to do the same. The journey up also gives you time to enjoy the great views over to the Bellevarde sector and up to La Grande Motte. At the top, the Madeleine and Manchet Express lifts are arriving just above you.

On arrival, you can leave either left or right. Dipping off to the left is the start of the short, wide Fourche red piste, which is merely a link down to join the Col de la Madeleine blue below. U-turning to either side after dismount begins the Marais blue piste, running parallel down the lift-line.

MARAIS

Although graded blue, this has a very mellow red profile top section before becoming a wide motorway cruise with two distinct routes. There are two start points, U-turning to either side of the Datcha chair lift, but both merge together lower under the lift-line to give the same possibilities from that point. Veering right takes you on a steeper fall-line schuss towards the Datcha restaurant and Cugnai chair lift; veering left involves a milder cruise linking you over to the Madeleine Express and Lac lifts, offering the best link towards Val d'Isère.

MADELEINE EXPRESS CHAIR LIFT

  4¼ mins

- 167 m (548 ft) vertical rise
- 905 m (990 yd) long
- 3000 passengers/hour

This is probably the best lift for early novices to begin exploring this sector, with stunning views towards La Grande Motte and a true high-altitude feel, plus a huge motorway green piste running back down under the lift-line to provide an ideal confidence-building first real piste. It is also handy for better intermediates to access the off-piste and lovely red and black cruises in the Manchet Valley.

On arrival, dismount to the right for the Madeleine green and for the Arcelle red and Marmottons black in the Manchet Valley; to the left is the start of the Col de la Madeleine blue, starting with a fairly steep pitch to merge with the St Jacques red below before flowing as a fast standard blue towards the Datcha restaurant area.

MADELEINE

Huge runway-wide green (really a mild blue) flowing straight back down the line of the Madeleine lift. A lovely, well-groomed proving ground for competent beginners making their first forays in the higher areas. The Manchet Express chair lift also arrives to the left of the piste about 100 m (109 yd) from the top; the pistes dropping off into the valley below are the Arcelle red and Marmottons black. The Madeleine makes a good link with the base of the chair lift again, as well as to the Lac chair lift and the l'Ouillette snack bar. The Lac chair provides the best link towards Val d'Isère.

ARCELLE

An enjoyable red that runs down the side of the Manchet Express
chair lift in the Manchet Valley and holds its condition well in the
afternoon. Approached via the Madeleine piste, the Arcelle is the
first run to start to the left. Drop in early for the steepest start on
this piste, which then swings left across the mountainside before
developing as a fair red overall. The Marmottons black is very
similar, but takes a slightly more direct line on the far side of
the lift. Both runs give plenty of opportunity to freeride off to
the sides and between the pistes, although riding out too wide
to the right can mean missing the otherwise good link with the
chair lift at the bottom.

MANCHET EXPRESS CHAIR LIFT

6³/₄ mins	• 700 m (2297 ft) vertical rise
	• 1921 m (2101 yd) long
	• 2400 passengers/hour

As well as serving the Arcelle and Marmottons pistes that run
down its sides, this lift provides a link for riders exiting from the
off-piste Le Manchet routes. If you miss the link, or if the lift stops
running, you can exit this area by taking the snowshoe/cross-
country circuit down to Le Châtelard.

The journey up this tranquil area gives great views up the
valley towards the impressive bulk of the Rocher du Charvet and
down towards Val d'Isère to the left. On arrival, U-turn to the right
for the Arcelle red (inclined); U-turn to the left for the Marmottons
black and a better link to the Arcelle. Alternatively, go straight off
and veer left to join the Madeleine green for all other routes and
links. Piste map, information board and tool point ahead.

LAC CHAIR LIFT

2¹/₂ mins

- 42 m (138 ft) vertical rise
- 226 m (247 yd) long
- 2400 passengers/hour

Caution – no footrest on safety bar. A slow-moving lift that serves to link the Leissières snowbowl to the top of the Solaise, for all onward routes towards Val d'Isère.

On arrival, go straight towards the Tête de Solaise restaurant area ahead, passing this on the left to take the Plan and Piste "M" reds, Piste "S" or Piste "A" blacks down to Val d'Isère base.

The Solaise chair lift arriving ahead to the right, above the restaurant, can be ridden down to Val d'Isère, as can the Solaise cable car that departs from the rear of the restaurant. Novices are advised to take a lift down.

L'OUILLETTE ROPE TOW

2¹/₂ mins ▲▼

- 3 m (10 ft) vertical rise
- 410 m (448 yd) long
- 1800 passengers/hour

Provides a tow along a flat section of the route between the Datcha restaurant area and the Lac chair lift, and vice versa. A poor link, nonetheless: coming from the Datcha restaurant towards Solaise the rope tow arrives around 10 m (11 yd) short of the Lac chair lift, necessitating a final slog, particularly for boarders. Travelling in the opposite direction is marginally better, because you can glide off to the left to begin descending towards the Glacier Express and Datcha chair lifts or towards Le Laisinant.

The best link towards Solaise and Val d'Isère involves taking the Datcha chair lift, then using the Madeleine green piste to reach the Lac chair lift more easily.

BELLEVARDE SKI SECTOR

The link between the Solaise and Bellevarde is the only one of Val d'Isère's sector interchanges not to happen at high altitude, involving a return to the valley and resort level.

The imposing bulk of the Rocher de Bellevarde dominates this sector. The famous Face black piste may have tamed the mountain, but there is nothing tame about the route itself on race days, and it remains the signature piste for the area. The upper sector is entwined with that of La Daille and has three routes making the home run towards Val d'Isère.

BELLEVARDE EXPRESS CHAIR LIFT

4	4³/₄ mins	• 384 m (1260 ft) vertical rise
		• 1000 m (1094 yd) long
		• 2400 passengers/hour

This accesses the slightly milder mid-point on the Face and makes a liaison with the Loyes Express chair lift to continue to the top of the Rocher de Bellevarde, passing the pleasant La Tanière mountain restaurant on the way.

The lift departs from the right-hand side of the l'Olympique cable car/swimming pool/sports complex at the base of the town slopes, and is reachable on-piste from both the Bellevarde and Solaise sides of the valley. On arrival, turn left for all pistes and to reach La Tanière restaurant, which is 20–25 m (22–27 yd) up a slight incline ahead. The blue link route over to the Loyes Express is both a ski link and a pedestrian route crossing the line of the Face run to reach the far side of the hill, and to access the Joseray red piste. Keep an eye out for traffic descending from above right.

◀ *Face de Bellevarde, Val d'Isère's Olympic course*

LOYES EXPRESS CHAIR LIFT

- 529 m (1736 ft) vertical rise
- 1445 m (1581 yd) long
- 2400 passengers/hour

This is the second half of the chair-lift journey up the Rocher de Bellevarde, and handy if you are content playing around the upper section of the Face black. It is an easy link traverse across from the Bellevarde Express chair lift and La Tanière restaurant. The Joseray red variation on the Face run starts to the left just before you reach the get-on level. Approach the chair lift from the far side of the lift-line for the best way to reach the control gates. The journey up gives good views over La Banane off-piste chutes to the left, and over the upper twists and turns of the Face run.

On arrival, dismount straight ahead and veer left. L'Olympique cable car arrives slightly above right. The Bellevarde restaurant is straight ahead. Head in this direction, too, to link into La Daille via the OK/Orange reds, Diebold/'3i' blues and Verte/Mont Blanc greens; and for the link to the Grand Pré area via the Collet blue. U-turn left for the Face black, or simply turn left for the Fontaine Froide red towards the Santons area.

PEDESTRIANS

Note that if you have journeyed up on the Loyes Express as a pedestrian, you will need to take the cable car or the Funival back down since this lift is one-way only. The Funival upper station is on the same level as l'Olympique cable car upper station, above right after arriving on this chair lift. Please take care in this area as it is a busy piste crossover point.

L'OLYMPIQUE CABLE CAR

6 mins

- 853 m (2799 ft) vertical rise
- 1932 m (2113 yd) long
- 3750 passengers/hour

When is a cable car not a cable car? When it is a giant gondola! This fantastic piece of engineering was only the second of its kind in the world when it was built in 2002. The cabins on this lift declutch from the main haul cable and operate just like a gondola, providing a continuous uplift. The lift also uses an innovative three-cable system (one haul and two load-bearing track cables) to allow a faster speed and excellent stability in windspeeds that would normally close other cable cars. This system also permitted a less environmentally invasive construction because the stronger cables required only three pylon sites between the lower and upper stations.

On arrival, leave the station straight ahead. The Funival upper station is on this same level, ahead right (there is also a first-aid point here). All routes begin immediately to the left: the Face black and Fontaine Froide red furthest left, a short slide to Le Bellevarde restaurant central right, and all other routes towards the Grande Pré area and La Daille, accessible by traversing across the rear of the restaurant.

🛈 Busy crossover point.

FACE

There are two entrances into the Face from the upper Bellevarde area, accessed to the left of the uppermost section of the Fontaine Froide red. Both access tracks are very mild and green in profile. The top section is wide and gentle, no more than blue in character, swinging left across the mountain to get to the highest, most central proper start for the run. There is plenty of inviting deeper and steeper stuff to the sides, but be warned that this is a seriously exposed off-piste zone, particularly to the right, so never proceed without first employing a local guide. The Face picks up pace to a fair red through the twists and turns of the upper pitches; the final sharp bend to the right narrows and can be very choppy once traffic builds up. The prime descent now begins, as a runway-wide superpiste belting almost straight down the mountainside. The piste is often mogulled, but is simply a very good red overall – its true power unleashed only when tackled at full tilt. It is easy to ride wide left at this upper mid-point to reach La Tanière restaurant for rest breaks or lunch; be careful if continuing straight down because you cross the line of the link piste/pedestrian route from the Bellevarde Express lift.

Keeping to the right will take you to the Loyes Express chair lift. This side also takes you to the start of the short Joseray red variation. The rocky outcrop just to the right of the cable car pylon, in the middle of the hill, is a lovely diversion, with boulder jumps and natural kickers. The main piste curves above the pylon and drops straight towards town. There is an interesting gully to the left, under the line of the chair lift; otherwise just schuss directly to the finish – keeping to the right for l'Olympique cable car back up to Bellevarde or the Solaise Express chair lift to link with the Solaise sector; keep left to access the Bellevarde Express chair lift.

FONTAINE FROIDE

This is a great warm-up red, beginning at the busy mass start area coming from the l'Olympique cable car and Funival. Descend to the left of the Bellevarde restaurant to follow the clear directional signage for this piste and towards the Santons blue and Épaule du Charvet black. The uppermost section passes the entrances for the Face black (departing to the left) as a standard blue, gradually increasing in gradient and picking up speed to a good fast red. The right-hand side of the piste has a pronounced lip that cries out for a launch off into the deeper stuff to the side. The piste is a fast motorway, with a couple of good, steep sections, making a great link with the Fontaine Froide chair lift on the bottom right; a fair link to the Santons twin button lifts ahead right. Alternatively, you can swing left to start the Santons blue immediately and, via the furthest flatter track, the Épaule du Charvet black.

FONTAINE FROIDE CHAIR LIFT

- 296 m (971 ft) vertical rise
- 1149 m (1257 yd) long
- 2400 passengers/hour

This is a handy chair lift for returning to the top of Bellevarde after a warm-up on the Fontaine Froide red, or for nervous novices wanting to avoid the fairly testing Santons blue route to reach Val d'Isère. On arrival, go left for the Diebold blue and the Orange and OK reds. Alternatively, dismount sharp right for the Bellevarde restaurant, Verte and Mont Blanc greens, Collet, Diebold and '3i' blues, Fontaine Froide red and Face black.

There is also a short magic carpet conveyor here (one-minute trip) to take you up to the Funival/l'Olympique stations.

COLLET

This gentle blue deserves a detailed look because it makes a decent link over to the Grand Pré chair lift, and because its route is a little ambiguous as shown on the piste map compared to how it is on the ground.

The start of the route is the wide, shared start area for the Diebold and '3i' blues and Verte and Mont Blanc greens, directly under the line of the arriving Fontaine Froide chair lift. The chair lift arriving on the higher ground ahead right is the Marmottes from the upper La Daille sector. The Diebold blue, and access towards the '3i' blue, is the first turn-off to the right, the second being the start of the Verte green and towards the Mont Blanc green. The Collet continues to hug the line of the chair lift towards a junction ahead, where a variation start to the Fontaine Froide red peels off to the left under the lift. Veer right for the Collet, which only now runs away from the lift-line.

The piste is a wide standard blue, but has a couple of mild steeper pitches to help build speed straight towards the good link with the Grand Pré chair lift. Approaching the lift get-on point, you can also swing left and join the lower Grand Pré green towards the base of the Santons button lifts and Fontaine Froide chair lift.

GRAND PRÉ CHAIR LIFT

6½ mins

- 224 m (735 ft) vertical rise
- 865 m (946 yd) long
- 2365 passengers/hour

Caution – no footrest on safety bar. This is the only lift to serve the Charvet area at the far side of this wide snowbowl above Val d'Isère and La Daille, serving the Grand Pré green and Club des Sports blue pistes, and indispensable for reaching one of Val d'Isère's classic off-piste routes, the Charvet Tour.

The lift journey up allows you to pick lines on the seriously steep ground beside the Club des Sports piste below the Rocher du Charvet, but note the unmarked cliffs.

On arrival, go straight on for the Charvet Tour (for experts only; mountain guide recommended), or turn right to begin the Grand Pré green and access the Club des Sports blue. The arrival area is flat and wide, allowing you to pause to take in the views over the beautifully barren, white desert beyond, and up to the imposing Pointe de la Sana soaring above it. The views back over the ski area are terrific, too. The Col de Fresse link with Tignes is ahead left, with the magnificent Mont Blanc on the horizon beyond. There is a tool point near the little stone hut by the fence at the start area.

🔺 *Top of Grand Pré chair lift, looking over the Col de Fresse towards Mont Blanc*

GRAND PRÉ

This is an excellent choice for progressing novices as part of a first big-mountain tour. The piste swings out wide to the left from the flat start area and rolls gently over the furthest reaches of this huge open snowbowl. A couple of S-bends take the sting out of the steeper mid-section. Intermediates can play off in the deeper snow-fields to the sides to take a steeper line. The route then swings down to the right to make a good link with the Grand Pré lift again.

The lower section, past the chair-lift get-on point, is an even wider, gentler motorway parallel to the line of the Santons button lifts, but it holds a treasure: a sweet little gully to the left in the form of a natural mini-halfpipe, which is great fun for all abilities. This final section of the run makes a good link with the Fontaine Froide chair lift and the Santons button lifts, as well as flowing towards the Santons blue and Épaule du Charvet black home runs to Val d'Isère.

⬤ *Fontaine Froide and Santons lifts area towards the Grand Pré*

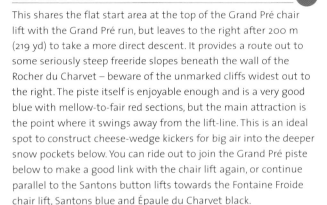

CLUB DES SPORTS

This shares the flat start area at the top of the Grand Pré chair lift with the Grand Pré run, but leaves to the right after 200 m (219 yd) to take a more direct descent. It provides a route out to some seriously steep freeride slopes beneath the wall of the Rocher du Charvet – beware of the unmarked cliffs widest out to the right. The piste itself is enjoyable enough and is a very good blue with mellow-to-fair red sections, but the main attraction is the point where it swings away from the lift-line. This is an ideal spot to construct cheese-wedge kickers for big air into the deeper snow pockets below. You can ride out to join the Grand Pré piste below to make a good link with the chair lift again, or continue parallel to the Santons button lifts towards the Fontaine Froide chair lift, Santons blue and Épaule du Charvet black.

SANTONS BUTTON LIFTS

  4 mins

- 149 m (489 ft) vertical rise
- 960 m (1050 yd) long
- 640 passengers/hour x 2

These are twin button lifts that make a good link with the Grand Pré chair lift and serve the lower sections of both the Club des Sports and Grand Pré pistes. The left-hand one rises slightly higher than the right-hand one, and often has a link track off to the left on arrival to join the Club des Sports, but there is no real advantage to be gained. Dismounting and turning right will take you down to the Grand Pré chair-lift get-on point.

At the point where the Grand Pré lift-line crosses above these button lifts, there is a great natural quarterpipe to the left when descending; stick high after dismounting to reach it.

ÉPAULE DU CHARVET

This is a short but diverting run begun from the area at the base of the Fontaine Froide and Santons lifts. The entrance is beside that of the Santons blue, on a high, flat track that is a real slog. There's plenty of opportunity to drop off the left-hand side into any powder above the Santons run; otherwise keep skating for the 400 or so metres (437 yd) it takes to clear the green profile traverse to reach the true start of the run. The piste drops straight over the shoulder of the hill, developing into a fair black, which is frequently mogulled. Unfortunately, the fun does not last long, because the route swings left to join the lower Santons blue for the long skate back to Val. It is also an east-facing slope in the full glare of the sun, so it is best early in the day. The views over the Le Manchet Valley are worth the effort of getting here, though.

SANTONS

The home-run blue from the Bellevarde sector is challenging for early novices at its upper section, and a real hike for its entire second half towards town. The start is wide but busy, and often very choppy, funnelling through a narrow gorge and developing a fair red character before emerging into the Manchet Valley and an increasingly mellower gradient, swinging left to run towards Val d'Isère on a long, flat track that winds its way through the chalet suburbs. Before it does, however, the route passes the attractive and good-quality Clochetons restaurant, so the best advice is to stop here for lunch or a reviving snifter. Then catch the ski bus back to Val d'Isère rather than skate – much more civilized.

▶ *View towards Val d'Isère and lower Solaise from the Épaule du Charvet*

LA DAILLE SKI SECTOR

This is the host sector for the Critérium de la Première Neige competition every year, and home to Val d'Isère's longest piste, La Verte (5 km/3 miles). As a satellite station a ski-bus ride or 20-minute walk away from Val d'Isère resort centre, La Daille is viewed as Val's budget option. It does, however, offer a very convenient base right at the heart of the Espace Killy, with a great range of peak-to-base fast reds and blues.

The surroundings are undeniably dramatic. There's a clump of huge, futuristic aparthotel blocks at the foot of a pair of sheer rock faces, which are even more impressive when spotlighted at night. Although there is little in the way of traditional Alpine charm, for accessibility and good, long cruising, La Daille scores.

BASE AREA

La Daille's best feature is that everything is within strolling distance. From the main accommodation complex it is only a few short steps out on to the base of the slopes, right beside the race-team huts and display boards listing the winners of all Première Neige and World Cup races held here since 1955 – once here, you are standing in the famous finish area. The Daille gondola is just ahead, while the Funival funicular is 150 m (164 yd) further on past the good Les Tufs piste-side restaurant.

From the main road, the approach to the open-air Funival base station is via a wide footbridge from the car park and ski bus stop (set down only) on the other side of the Isère River.

The massive accommodation blocks have a small commercial centre at their core, housing a good supermarket, equipment

◀ *Les Tufs restaurant at La Daille base*

rental and sales, launderette, the tourist office, fashion boutique, public telephones, snack bar, patisserie, bar and a couple of plain but functional restaurants.

The ski bus stop to and from Val d'Isère is just across the footbridge at the far side of the centre's car park.

All major pistes flow down into the base area to within a few metres of the lifts. The ski pass sales kiosks are just beside the Funival.

BEGINNERS' ZONE

The ski school meeting points are at the main base slopes, but the designated beginners' area is over on the far side of the Funival station. This 'Les Lanches' area has quieter wooded slopes served by two button lifts (free lifts – no ski pass required) and is safely away from the busy base pistes. Although the zone is very limited, it's certainly adequate for the first few days and once novices are competent enough to move out on to the mountain, there is a great range of long, green pistes in a beautiful open snowbowl accessible from the top of the Funival.

For children, there is a reasonably attractive Snow Garden in the landscaped grounds of the apartment complex nearest the slopes, equipped with a mini rope tow, colourful obstacles and cartoon statues.

DAILLE GONDOLA LIFT

- 495 m (1624 ft) vertical rise
- 1674 m (1831 yd) long
- 900 passengers/hour

This old, slow gondola (built in 1967) used to be the primary access point from La Daille base. The journey up gives good views over the lower sections of the La Daille home runs below.

On arrival, exit to the left to emerge on the big La Folie Douce bar and restaurant terrace. There is a fun and buzzing atmosphere here on sunny days, so it may be tempting to linger. Walk straight off the terrace and turn right to ride around the rear of the building and join the Verte green and link with the Mont Blanc chair lift to the Snow Park, or the fast Tommeuses chair lift linking with Tignes. Alternatively, walk straight off the terrace and go slightly uphill to be able to ride away down to the left to join all other lower routes towards La Daille base.

ETROITS CHAIR LIFT

 11½ mins

- 516 m (1693 ft) vertical rise
- 1690 m (1849 yd) long
- 1800 passengers/hour

This is another older lift taking a parallel line to the Daille gondola lift and arriving at a very similar altitude.

On arrival, dismount to the right to ride to La Folie Douce restaurant, keeping high above and to the left of the restaurant and gondola complex for the Verte green, and to link with the Mont Blanc and Tommeuses chair lifts. Alternatively, U-turn down to join the OK red for all other lower La Daille routes.

The Criterium blue also starts at the arrival point and descends to the right of the chair lift's pylon-line.

FUNIVAL FUNICULAR

- 908 m (2979 ft) vertical rise
- 2300 m (2516 yd) long
- 3000 passengers/hour

Inaugurated in 1987, this was the first mountain funicular of its type in France. It is a great piece of engineering and one of the prime access points for the Espace Killy, linking La Daille directly with the top of the Rocher de Bellevarde for immediate access into both the Bellevarde and La Daille sectors. Although there is just a single track, there are actually two trains; the track splits at the mid-point inside the tunnel (1760 m/1925 yd long) so that the synchronized descending train can pass.

Once up the short flight of steps through the base station ski-pass control, you come out directly on to the open-air plat-form, rising in wide, stepped stages up either side of the track; you can board from either side. There are tool points on both sides of the platform.

The floors of the two carriages that make up the train have a considerable forward pitch, making it awkward to stand upright here at the base station, but as the train climbs up the ever-increasing gradient into the tunnel, the floor angle becomes horizontal. There are a number of solid upright rests for leaning on to make it easier to stand.

On arrival, dismount to either side and exit straight ahead up the stepped platforms of the upper station building: there are WCs, a piste map and tool points just before the exit.

Outside, the flat, pisted arrival zone is really busy, so leave the area swiftly. The OK and Orange red pistes begin immediately to the right, with access to the Diebold and "3i" blues, heading in the direction of the Snow Park and Tignes. For all other routes go left.

ORIENTATION

From the Funival arrival area there are great sweeping views over this whole snowbowl where the Bellevarde and La Daille sectors intertwine. Directly ahead you are looking towards the Rocher du Charvet, with the peak of the Pointe de la Sana beyond; on a clear day you can make out the glacier pistes on Tignes' La Grande Motte ahead right, with the sheer wall of the massive 3852 m (12,638 ft) La Grande Casse just beyond. The Borsat Express and Tommeuses chair lifts effecting the link with Tignes are the two lifts rising up the arête to your far right. To your left, you are looking over to Val d'Isère's upper Solaise sector on the far side of the Manchet Valley. Looking down over the fence ahead, the Bellevarde restaurant is just below. The magic carpet conveyor rising diagonally in front of you is providing a link up from the top of the Fontaine Froide chair lift, which is arriving below right. The Orange and OK red pistes start to your immediate right.

Turning left, past the ski-patrol first-aid hut, you continue on this flat pisted level towards Val d'Isère's l'Olympique cable-car station to get to the shared start for the Fontaine Froide red and all routes to Val d'Isère; also to access the Bellevarde restaurant below; and to run to the right behind the restaurant for the Collet, Diebold and "3i" blues, Verte and Mont Blanc greens.

🔺 *Bellevarde restaurant area*

OK

This is La Daille's signature run and route of the Critérium de la Première Neige race course. The OK and Orange share the same start from the Funival arrival level. It is a narrow entrance, and the piste quickly gets chopped up. Stay central – leaving to the left links over to the Diebold and "3i" blues. The piste flattens considerably, so keep momentum up from the initial steep start. Bear left at the next junction ahead; highest right is the Orange. The OK now continues as a wide mild red, sweeping right towards La Folie Douce restaurant/Daille gondola station. The whole mountainside is pisted and open, allowing variant lines in most directions. The Mont Blanc chair lift to the Snow Park and the Tommeuses chair lift to Tignes are easy to reach ahead left. To stay fast and out of any busy traffic, go to the right of the Etroits chair lift to share the slope with the Criterium blue down the pylon-line.

La Daille is now visible below. The views also open up to the right around the side of the Rocher de Bellevarde, giving you a clear line of sight towards Val d'Isère and Le Fornet. There is a junction 500 m (547 yd) ahead. Keep right for the OK; left takes you to the Diebold blue and Piste "G" black. Follow the line of the gondola for a now much steeper good red, eventually veering left into the clearing in front of Le Triffolet restaurant. The piste map is hard to follow at this point because the routes and crossover points are all intertwined. The OK goes to the right of the copse of trees at the end of the clearing, finally schussing fast into the race finish area at La Daille beside the gondola station; go high to the right under the lift lines to reach the Etroits chair lift.

If you want to reach the Funival, you need to traverse off to the right at the Triffolet restaurant level to join the Diebold and Verte on the flat track through the trees.

ORANGE

The uppermost section is shared with the OK, dropping from the Funival arrival level as a short, steep speed-builder before veering away flatter from the OK to stay higher to the right. The piste follows a gentle contour-line route around the back of the Rocher de Bellevarde, but there are plenty of opportunities to drop off to the left for a steeper ride down to join the OK below.

The piste then begins to build speed, the gradient improving as you head into the tree line. The woods here are perfectly spaced for a spot of glade-riding down to the left to join the other main pistes below. Alternatively, remain high on the Orange for the steepest part of the piste itself. The lower section narrows through the wooded slopes and drops out to merge with the Verte green and Criterium blue, flowing together on the wide base slopes for good links with the Funival base station on the right or Le Tufs restaurant to the left.

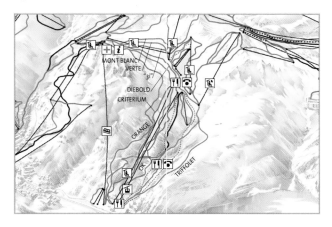

CRITERIUM

In effect, this is simply the milder twin lower section of the OK red, sharing the wide, open slopes below the Etroits lift-line. Once you reach the tree line, the OK leaves to the left and the Criterium stays high to the right with the line of the chair lift for a pleasant but often choppy route through the woods. The Diebold blue and Verte green then join from the left, at a crossover point where the Verte trail cuts across from left to right to take the flattest route through the woods. The merged Criterium/Diebold piste continues down the fall-line with a mild-to-fair red profile, with lots of variations possible around the tree clumps. Finish is via the wide slopes towards the Funival base station and Les Tufs restaurant.

DIEBOLD & "3i"

The entrance to these is from behind the Bellevarde restaurant, traversing under the line of the arriving Fontaine Froide chair lift to continue straight on parallel to the line of the three-seater Marmottes chair lift. This section is shared with the start of the Verte and Mont Blanc greens, which peel off to the left, whilst the Diebold and "3i" veer right towards a junction point of their own; the "3i" bears to the left and flows straightest and fastest towards the Marmottes restaurant area (for the Marmottes and Borsat Express lifts and the Snow Park).

The Diebold curves higher to the right towards La Folie Douce. Passing in front of the restaurant, the route continues down the wide shared hillside, now veering to the left of the gondola pylon-line. There is a choice ahead: continue into the clearing at the Triffolet restaurant area ahead left, or join with the Criterium blue through the woods towards La Daille base as described above.

VERTE & MONT BLANC

The Verte has the distinction of being Val d'Isère's longest piste, running a full 5 km (3 miles) from Bellevarde to La Daille. Really a good blue run, it also holds a couple of surprises, which even advanced riders will appreciate. The Mont Blanc is basically a shorter twin. Access to both is from the Bellevarde restaurant area, at an entrance shared with the Diebold and "3i" blues (see opposite). The Mont Blanc peels off to the left after 100 m (109 yd), swinging wide and gently into the middle of the snow-bowl. The Verte goes straight on. Both pistes splice together again approaching the Marmottes restaurant area, where the Mont Blanc terminates. The Verte runs past the restaurant and is joined from above left by the Edelweiss blue at the end of the Snow Park; veer left to link with the Mont Blanc chair lift, or stick to the higher ground to the right.

There is a huge natural halfpipe, with a good gradient and high side walls, bang in the middle of these two routes. This playground runs for about 350 m (383 yd) and exits just below the Mont Blanc chair lift, rejoining the Verte for a good link with the Tommeuses chair lift for Tignes. The Verte then swings down to the right, to where the Trifollet red piste begins over a bridge to the left.

The deep gorge below is known as the Vallée Perdue (the Lost Valley) and is a wonderful opportunity for more advanced riders to do a spot of Indiana Jones touring (see page 130).

The Verte veers right and into a tunnel under the Piste "G" black, merging with the "G" on the far side and flowing into a wide clearing in front of the Triffolet restaurant. The trail is picked up again by following the signs off to the right, on a narrow track through the woods to take the gentlest contour-line route down to the Funival at La Daille base below.

VALLÉE PERDUE

The Lost Valley! It is easily discoverable again, and is an interesting diversion for competent intermediates and above. The valley is the deep torrent gorge of the Tovière River, entered by dropping off down its steep, snow-laden sides near the skiable bridge at the junction for the Triffolet red route off the Verte green: keep wide to the left of the Semanmille button lift, using the Verte green to get here.

The steep drop in is the tricky bit, with a 60-degree angle at most points – simply pick your line and go for it. Once on the flat floor of the gorge, you run down between the impressive sheer rock walls on a winding, narrow and deeply shadowed corridor, exiting near the Triffolet restaurant and back to civilization.

TRIFFOLET

In good snow conditions, this fair red at the far side of the ski area is worth a go, but the low altitude and lack of snowmaking takes its toll, and the route is often closed or poorly maintained.

The run begins by crossing a skiable bridge to the left from the Verte green piste, before the Semanmille button lift. Across the bridge, over the 'Vallée Perdue', the route swings to the right, past the abandoned Chalets de la Tovière. This upper section is quite mellow, but it picks up momentum down this far flank of the river gorge, steepening up to a decent gradient and running under the cliffs of the Rocher du Saut, behind the Triffolet restaurant.

The route follows the line of a summer hiking trail and the surroundings are peaceful and quite wild. The steepest lower pitch veers right to join the Raye red for the final schuss into La Daille base area, towards the gondola station.

PISTE "G"

The piste "G" black and Raye red are spliced together to form
a complete descent on the fastest fall-line to La Daille. This line
traces the competition course here at La Daille. When events
barriers are dismantled it is quite difficult to follow the route,
since the upper section traverses the open and indistinctly shared
slopes below the gondola station. The run begins at the top of the
Semanmille lift, a short, steep button lift, which serves this open
hillside behind the gondola and restaurant building. To pick up
the route of the "G", head for the trees below the gondola's third
pylon; the signage here is poor – merely pointers in the general
direction of each route rather than any specific piste markings.
Swing left on the fall-line towards the trees to enter a much more
defined route lined with catch netting (there are some invitingly
steep glades here to the left, dropping out to the Verte some
distance below).

The Verte crosses from
below left, through a tunnel
under the "G", to merge more
safely on the right. In the
clearing ahead, in front of
the Triffolet restaurant, the
race line now becomes
known as the Raye, continuing the descent nearest to
the restaurant. Keep left for
the steepest line and an
often choppy and mogulled
good red pitch towards the
final schuss into the base area.

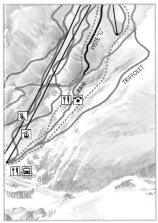

MARMOTTES CHAIR LIFT

9 mins

- 257 m (843 ft) vertical rise
- 1265 m (1384 yd) long
- 1800 passengers/hour

Caution – no footrest on safety bar. This is a slow, fixed chair lift providing uplift from the Marmottes restaurant area to the Bellevarde restaurant level, useful for reaching the Bellevarde sector to head towards Val d'Isère, and for novices to make circuits on the wide greens and blues running down either side of the lift-line through this lovely snowbowl.

The chair lift passing overhead is the Borsat Express, the roofing/netting above you giving protection from any falling objects. There is a tool point at the departure area.

On arrival, dismount straight ahead for the Collet blue and Fontaine Froide red, or turn left for the Verte and Mont Blanc greens and the Diebold and '3i' blues. The Bellevarde restaurant is just ahead, but a short skate is required to reach it.

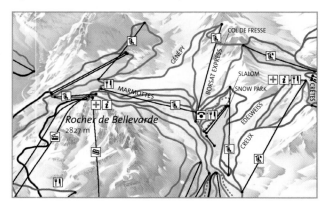

BORSAT EXPRESS CHAIR LIFT

8 mins

- 376 m (1234 ft) vertical rise
- 2084 m (2280 yd) long
- 2400 passengers/hour

This is the uppermost chair lift in La Daille, serving some lovely sweeping motorways accessible by all abilities, including the Col de Fresse ridge route linking to Tignes' Val Claret sector. Look out for the two lovely, natural halfpipes just after passing over the Marmottes chair lift; reach them via the lower Col de Fresse green. The runway-wide piste parallel to your left is the Borsat.

At the top, dismount straight ahead out on to the wide, flat arrival area; the views are worth pausing for. After just 10 m (11 yd), all three green pistes from here begin by dipping off to the left.

Advanced (fit) riders can hike up to the top of the ridge above right to drop into an off-piste descent and join the Tignes pistes below. The view from this ridge is great. Not only have you got the whole of the upper La Daille and Bellevarde sectors behind you, but you also have a clear view towards Val Claret ahead right. To the left you are looking straight up the flanks of La Grande Motte, with Tignes' Génépy and Cairn blues running down into the valley.

GÉNÉPY

This wide motorway begins alongside the Col de Fresse and Borsat greens. The first exit to the left is the Col de Fresse, the second is the Borsat. The Génépy takes an arrow-straight line ahead, flowing gently towards a good link with the Grand Pré chair lift and onwards as the Grand Pré green to the Fontaine Froide/Santons lifts. You can also continue descending all the way to Val d'Isère via the Santons blue.

COL DE FRESSE

From the top of the Borsat Express chair lift, the Col de Fresse route takes the first, highest branch off to the left, U-turning to run under the lift cables and hugging the contour-line to traverse wide out to the left towards the saddle of the Col de Fresse itself.

As you approach the col and the arrival point of Val Claret's Fresse chair lift, you can crest the ridge to begin the Isolée blue run to the left, effecting the link into Tignes (see page 213). The Prariond blue on the far side of the lift is reached only after an inclined slope and there is no real advantage in choosing it.

Remaining on the Val d'Isère side of the col, the route veers down to the right on this still-gentle Col de Fresse piste (caution for traffic joining from the Fresse chair lift), eventually sweeping down under the line of the Borsat Express lift and joining the Verte piste towards the Marmottes restaurant area.

There are plenty of opportunities for those with more competent abilities to ride off the lip on the right side of the piste and through the huge open expanse of deeper powder in this upper bowl, but the terrain is quite gentle and can require a hike to get out of if you lose momentum.

A detour not to miss, though, are the huge, natural halfpipes above the Marmottes restaurant area. To reach them, stay on the Col de Fresse piste until just before you go under the first chair-lift line ahead (Borsat Express), then ride off to the left. Just below, there is a pair of long gullies running parallel to each other, and parallel to the line of the rising chair lift. With natural kickers to launch in off and high side walls to play on, they should be on every freerider's list. The pipes exit just above the Marmottes restaurant area, near the get-on point for the Marmottes chair lift; they can be seen from the restaurant terrace and both chair lifts.

SLALOM & SNOW PARK BUTTON LIFTS

2½ mins

- 103 m (338 ft) vertical rise
- 350 m (383 yd) long
- 900 passengers/hour x 2

These twin, retracting reel-cord button lifts depart from the area just below the get-on point for the Borsat Express chair lift, behind and below the Marmottes restaurant. As the names suggest, they serve the public slalom stadium and the Snow Park.

You can take either lift because they run parallel and arrive at the same height, although the left-hand one is best for accessing the slalom course.

At the top, the chair lift arriving above left is the Mont Blanc; the Tines blue piste coming from it also passes this arrival point and continues down to your right. Either turn immediately right for the top entrance into the Snow Park's big air tables, or ride with the Tines piste towards the next entrance for the Boarder/SkierCross course. Alternatively, turn left into the start of the slalom stadium.

SLALOM

The Slalom piste is a public-access, pay-to-use slalom stadium, which is equipped with a computerized, infra-red timing system. The stadium is open to 'amateurs' from 09.30–14.00 hours.

The course costs a couple of euros per descent – you pay at the exit cabin after your run. There is a large digital stop-clock at the finish area for checking your time and speed, plus a display board where the day's best times are posted.

The stadium can also be reached using the Mont Blanc chair lift and leaving to the right on the Tines blue.

● *Towards the Snow Park chill zone*

SNOW PARK

Val d'Isère's only tricks park is situated near the Marmottes restaurant in the upper La Daille sector, best reached by approaching from the top of the Bellevarde area.

From La Daille base, take the Funival and ride down to link with the Snow Park drag lift or the Mont Blanc chair lift. From Val d'Isère, use the Olympique cable car to do the same. From Tignes, take the Edelweiss blue from Tovière. You can also get here via the Col de Fresse from Val Claret.

The park is set out in a lateral fashion across the hill, therefore does not give a very long in-line run, but at least it has a fair selection of modules so that you can keep taking different lines through the zone for a different run each time. Although primarily aimed at experienced riders, there are a few mellower training modules for novices to practise on before hitting the main park.

SNOW PARK FEATURES

Modules include a permanent halfpipe, two quarters (facing each other), a couple of big air tables, a number of mid-height tables, some smaller training tables, a range of hips, a rainbow, a flat box, a couple of flat-down rails, plus a couple of simple rails. Additionally, there is a mid-sized Boarder/SkierCross course running round the perimeter.

A chill zone over by the rails area has a riders' cabin, equipped with a webcam (🅦 www.viewsurf.com / 🅦 www.valdisere.com), repair bench and tool point, computer terminal for uploading the best shots from your digital camera, barbeque and music system.

The park is best served by the Mont Blanc chair lift, although there are no footrests on the safety bar so it is a bit awkward to use. There is also a rope tow that runs along the base of the zone (The Bozetto) but it is a long slog for the 1¼ minutes it takes to ride it, and it makes a poor link with the Snow Park/Slalom button lifts anyway.

It is best to ride out of the park towards the Mont Blanc chair lift, which takes you past the big natural halfpipe to the side of the lower Edelweiss blue piste, so it is more fun and extends your riding time.

🔺 *Grabbing air in Val's Snow Park*

MONT BLANC CHAIR LIFT

  9 mins

- 257 m (843 ft) vertical rise
- 1108 m (1212 yd) long
- 1800 passengers/hour

Caution – no footrest on safety bar. This old, slow chair serves the Snow Park and provides a link to the Marmottes restaurant, as well as to the Marmottes and Borsat Express chair lifts. Beware of the vicious kick to the chair at the get-on point – Val d'Isère really needs to upgrade to a decent lift to serve its tricks park!

The journey up gives you a good bird's-eye view over the park, though, giving you time to pick your line through the various modules within it. Note that there are two entrances into the park, the lower one leading in closer to the Border/SkierCross course.

On arrival, either turn left to drop down on the short and steepish Moutons blue piste down to the Marmottes restaurant, and to link with the Marmottes and (best) Borsat Express chair lift, or U-turn right to start the Tines blue for the short ride down to the top of the Snow Park and slalom stadium.

⬤ *Panorama over the Snow Park and Marmottes restaurant area*

TOMMEUSES CHAIR LIFT

7½ mins

- 460 m (1509 ft) vertical rise • Last lift up 16.45
- 1716 m (1877 yd) long
- 4000 passengers/hour

Strictly speaking, this fast, eight-seater chair lift belongs to Tignes, but since it is based in La Daille sector it makes more sense to include it here. It provides access to all the runs on this side of Tovière peak and to make on-piste links directly with Tignes-Le-Lac and Val Claret; approach via the Verte green or the Creux blue. There is a magic carpet conveyor at the get-on point, making things even quicker.

At the top, you arrive directly onto a compact plateau just below the summit, at a busy lifts junction and restaurant area. The Tovière restaurant (see page 261) is on your left, Tignes' Aeroski gondola is straight ahead and to the right there is a large ski-patrol cabin, and information, first-aid and tool point. Turn immediately left to access the Crêtes and Rocs reds, which U-turn under the lift-line, or to run around to the front of the restaurant to access all other pistes. The Pâquerettes black freeride route (see page 218) is accessed by taking the flat, narrow track along the far side of the Aeroski.

◆ Tignes' eight-seater Tommeuses chair lift, linking from La Daille mid-sector to Tovière peak

CRÊTES

This is a short ridge run from Tovière to the arrival point of Tignes' Combe Folle button lift. The whole mountainside to the right is an invitingly open and superb powder ride, eventually joining the Creux blue below. Sticking to the ridge, once you reach the col where the lift is arriving, you have two choices. Either drop to the right to take the Violettes blue (mild-to-fair red) linking with the Creux blue towards La Daille, or turn left over the col on to the short but decent Combe Folle red towards Tignes-le-Lac.

CREUX & EDELWEISS

This is good cruising with some mild red characteristics. Both routes share the same wide start area with Tignes' Piste "H" blue, flowing away from the Tovière restaurant terrace. Veer left following the clear, centrally positioned piste signage towards La Daille and Val d'Isère. Where the pistes next split, keep right for the Edelweiss or veer left for the Creux. The Edelweiss is the best choice for reaching the Snow Park and lifts to the upper sectors. Nearing the line of the Mont Blanc chair lift, it is joined from the right by the Tines blue piste; both skirt the perimeter of the Snow Park, down to make a good link with the Mont Blanc lift.

The Creux is more or less a twin, but sweeps out across the mountainside to be joined from above by the two enjoyable steeper Rocs red pistes and the Violettes blue. Note that there is a wide gully separating this piste from the Mont Blanc lift get-on point (the gully is good fun to play in, though!), but it does link well with the Tommeuses chair lift back up to Tovière again.

▶ *La Daille, looking towards Solaise and Crêtes des Leissières*

POINT-TO-POINT ROUTES: COMPETENT NOVICES

VAL D'ISÈRE » PISSAILLAS GLACIER

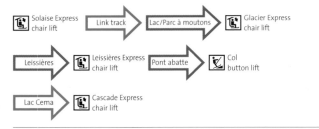

PISSAILLAS GLACIER » VAL D'ISÈRE

VAL D'ISÈRE » VAL CLARET (TIGNES)

VAL CLARET (TIGNES) » VAL D'ISÈRE

VAL D'ISÈRE » TIGNES-LE-LAC

TIGNES-LE-LAC » VAL D'ISÉRE

LA DAILLE » TOVIÈRE (TIGNES LINK)

TOVIÈRE (TIGNES LINK) » LA DAILLE

VAL D'ISÈRE » VAL CLARET CENTRE

VAL CLARET CENTRE » VAL D'ISÈRE – SEE PAGES 254–255

POINT-TO-POINT ROUTES: GOOD INTERMEDIATES AND ABOVE

VAL D'ISÈRE » PISSAILLAS GLACIER

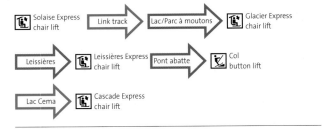

Solaise Express chair lift → Link track → Lac/Parc à moutons → Glacier Express chair lift

Leissières → Leissières Express chair lift → Pont abatte → Col button lift

Lac Cema → Cascade Express chair lift

PISSAILLAS GLACIER » VAL D'ISÈRE

Cema chair lift → Pont Abatte → Leissières Express chair lift → Plan Milet

Datcha chair lift → Marais → Lac chair lift → Plan → Piste "M"

VAL D'ISÈRE » TIGNES-LE-LAC

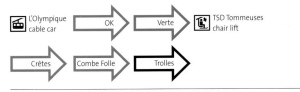

L'Olympique cable car → OK → Verte → TSD Tommeuses chair lift

Crêtes → Combe Folle → Trolles

TIGNES-LE-LAC » VAL D'ISÈRE

Aeroski gondola → Edelweiss → OK → Diebold → Funival funicular → Face

VAL D'ISÈRE » VAL CLARET (TIGNES)

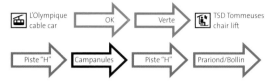

VAL CLARET (TIGNES) » VAL D'ISÈRE

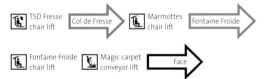

LA DAILLE » TOVIÈRE (TIGNES LINK)

TOVIÈRE (TIGNES LINK) » LA DAILLE

VAL D'ISÈRE » VAL CLARET CENTRE

VAL CLARET CENTRE » VAL D'ISÈRE – SEE PAGE 257

MOUNTAIN BARS & RESTAURANTS

Despite the expansive extent of the ski domain, in virtually all sectors of Val d'Isère you are never more than one piste and/or one lift away from a mountain bar or restaurant. Many are either snack bars or busy, self-service canteen-style restaurants, where it can be a bit of a scrum for seating and choice in high season, but there are also a number of quality establishments offering more refined gastronomic fare and ambiance, and accepting table bookings.

Most venues open for lunch from around noon to 15.00 hours, but offer an all-day bar and snack service; all but the smallest snack bars have WCs – most of these are serviced and levy a small charge.

LE FORNET SECTOR

There are just two on-mountain restaurants in this high and wild sector, plus a couple of options at the base area.

Les Crozets €€ This is a basic self-service cafeteria on the lower ground floor of the Fornet cable-car base station; almost piste-side but with an inclined slope from the end of Le Fornet's home runs. The small terrace has some deckchairs and patio tables and chairs, with views over the approaching pistes, looking straight up the lift-line and lower section of the Forêt black piste.

This is a plain, seventies-style canteen, offering an all-day bar service plus a basic lunchtime self-service buffet heavily centred on fast food. It is open until 18.00 hours, so handy for an immediate après-ski snifter or hot drink, although the lovely rustic **Auberge l'Arolay**, a short walk down the road at the entrance to the old hamlet, is much nicer and more atmospheric.

◄ *Les Clochetons restaurant, Bellevarde sector, Val d'Isère*

Le Signal €€ Situated beside the shared Fornet cable car/Vallon de l'Iseran gondola station at 2330 m (7645 ft), at the base of the Vallon and Pré-chemin blue runs. This venue is famous for its cosy Mongolian yurt on the terrace, complete with roaring log fire and bar. The terrace has great views down the valley towards Val and La Daille. It has its own snack-bar kiosk serving hot and cold drinks, hot dogs, soup and filled baguettes. There are quite a few bench-style tables and seating, plus deckchairs.

Inside at the terrace level, there is a cosy small bar and self-service restaurant offering a fair selection of basic salads, hors d'oeuvres, hot dishes and canned and bottled drinks. The interior is old-fashioned but pleasant; the valley side of the building has large picture windows and good views.

Stairs lead up to an attractive small à la carte restaurant; the room is cosy and rustic, with plenty of natural light from windows overlooking the valley. Fare on offer is of a good quality, with oysters, fish, tartiflette and meat dishes, plus a very good wine list. This level also has its own separate terrace with table service and, on fair-weather days, an open-air buffet. ☎ +33 (0)4 79 06 03 38

Chalet Edelweiss €€ A recent and welcome addition to the on-mountain venues in this sector, in a peaceful elevated spot overlooking the woods towards Val d'Isère. Ski-to-terrace site on the lower Mangard blue piste, just past the junction for the Cognon red piste. Large Savoyard chalet-style building of quality construction and decor; airy and attractive interior plus waiter-served terrace; some sunloungers available.

Good range of entrées and a short but select menu of main courses, including tartiflette and a range of tagliatelles and refined meat-based dishes. ☎ +33 (0)6 10 28 70 64

SOLAISE SECTOR

As the core of Val d'Isère's original ski domain, the Solaise has always been a major focus for on-piste lunch. However, this does mean that the venues get very busy and, despite their popularity, the fare on offer can be a bit bland.

Datcha € This is sited in the middle of the big snowbowl in the upper Solaise sector, just by the get-on point for the Cugnai chair lift; accessible from the Plan Milet, Glacier, Col de Madeleine, Fourche and Marais pistes, as well as using l'Ouillette rope tow if coming from the top of the Solaise. It is a reasonably attractive stone-built chalet, with a good-sized decked terrace facing directly south-east with views up the snowbowl. A small self-service restaurant is inside with a fair range of canned and bottled drinks and simple hot dishes and snack foods, including sausages and chips, quiche, spaghetti and salads; full bar service at small separate bar within this main interior saloon.

A separate compact dining room, with plain but pleasant wood-clad decor, offers a plat du jour special plus a limited but decent à la carte selection and a fair range of wines.

L'Ouillette € Quaint little refuge in a lovely position overlooking the frozen l'Ouillette Lake and the Nordic/snowshoes circuits, between the Lac and Madeleine Express chair lifts. Attractive wood-decked terrace overlooking the lake and Madeleine piste, with views towards the Rocher du Charvet and La Grande Motte. Full bar service and snack bar menu, including a plat du jour, a range of salads, tartiflette, hot dogs, filled baguettes and soup. There is also a tiny interior dining room with a slightly more involved menu. Fair range of Savoie wines and vin chaud available.

Tête de Solaise €€ This sector's main catering focus is hard to miss because it is plonked almost on the summit of the Solaise, in the same building as the Solaise cable-car station.

The terrace is huge and normally buzzing with both skiers and non-skiers; it is waiter-served for drinks only. There are a couple of fast-food kiosks on the terrace that offer crêpes and full-sized hand-thrown pizzas. A microwave oven is provided by the main restaurant entrance for reheating food that is cooling too quickly.

Inside, there is a separate large bar area to the left, which is cosy enough for such an open space. Ahead right is the main self-service food selection area, which has a staffed bar counter and offers a good selection of ready-made salads, hot combination dishes, set menus, daily specials, pizzas, fresh fruit and a good range of simple desserts plus a wide range of bottled and canned drinks. A huge interior dining and seating area occupies the entire far side of the building.

⬤ *The buzzing terrace at the Tête de Solaise restaurant*

Another option is to come down off the mountain and return to base for lunch; Val d'Isère's Front de Neige area terraces are always buzzing with skiers and non-skiers from lunchtime to mid-afternoon, and the long square running towards the town centre from between the Brussels and Grand Paradis hotels makes it easy to get as close as possible to the resort centre.

Hotel Brussels €€ This has the biggest presence in the town's base area, with a huge terrace furnished with masses of deckchairs and a snack kiosk.

Hotel Grand Paradis and Le Schuss restaurant €€+ Just opposite the Brussels, these have better quality menus and attractive piste-side/road-side, wind-shielded terraces.

Café des Sports/Brasserie de Grand Cours €€ A popular venue for instructors and saisonnaires; a bit old-fashioned, but serves a good range of carbohydrate-loaded fare.

La Tartine € Located at the lower right-hand corner of the square, this is an excellent little fast-food counter, with delicious home-baked quiches, tartlets, paninis and rarebits.

La Grande Ourse €€€ Back up at the main slope-side terraces, this has a front-line position near the Savonnette button lifts and a offers refined quality *menu du jour*.

Bananas €€ Situated at the lowest corner of the main base area, this is just about reachable with your gear on. Tex-Mex and energy-boosting pastas and a cool, young vibe. Heated terrace.

BELLEVARDE SECTOR

There are only three venues to talk about on the Val d'Isère side of the Bellevarde, but they are all good. All have great views and one is bang in the middle of the Face de Bellevarde Olympic piste, yet can be reached by visitors of all abilities, whether skiers or not.

Bellevarde €€ The signature restaurant for this sector, situated just below the upper stations of both the Funival and l'Olympique cable car. There is a large sun terrace with views over this wide and open snowbowl to the Rocher du Charvet, and across the valley towards Cugnai and the Crête des Leissières; it also has some deckchairs. The terrace has table service for drinks, and drinks and snacks are available from a service counter at the front of the building. Inside there are two floors: on the main ground floor terrace level there is a large bar and self-service dining saloon; the self-service selection area is at the rear. Fare on offer is a standard range of pastas, omelettes, chicken and chips, and so on. Microwaves are available for reheating food. The decor is a bit plain, but not unattractive, with plenty of natural wood; bench seating and tables are refectory-style. A separate smaller room to the left of the food selection area is perfect for groups.

Upstairs, there is a very attractive and welcoming large à la carte restaurant, with its own wind-shielded balcony and an interior upper mezzanine. This is decorated in alpine chalet style, with high-pitched ceiling and exposed wooden beams around a central log fireplace. As well as the good-quality à la carte fare focused on Savoyard specialities, such as potée and fondue, there is a good range of set menus and an excellent 'buffet Savoyard' with choice of salads, hors d'oeuvres, soup, charcuterie, cheese and desserts. ☏ +33 (0)4 79 06 05 76

La Tanière €€ Cosy, attractive venue in a great position slap bang in the middle of the Face de Bellevarde, ski-to-door and a short glide or stroll from the top of the Bellevarde Express chair lift.

There is a compact snow terrace with some deckchairs and superb views straight across to the Solaise and up the valley towards Le Fornet and the peaks beyond. There are no gear racks, so be sure your gear is positioned safely. Full bar and restaurant service in the snug interior, which also has an upper mezzanine.

The menu is fairly extensive and the fare is of good quality, with a refined choice and a decent wine selection. The venue is available for evening bookings and events: by arrangement you can order kir royale on arrival, buffet Savoyard, fondue, fireworks and a torchlight descent on the Face (good skiers only); minimum of 10 persons required. ☎ +33 (0)6 20 63 76 97

Les Clochetons €€+ This is a large Savoyard-style chalet, which is the last building in town at Le Châtelard; accessible by car, on foot, by ski bus and by piste (Santons blue run). The Manchet Valley Nordic and snowshoe circuits also depart from here.

Large sunny terrace with plenty of deckchairs and a great view up the Manchet Valley; snack bar kiosk on terrace plus waited service from restaurant for terrace dining tables. The double-height interior is bright and airy, with quality decor using plenty of natural stone and wood. Full bar, chef-attended open-fire grill, and attractive large ground floor dining saloon and mezzanine.

Extensive, good-quality lunch menu featuring a number of fish dishes as well as wood-fire grills and roast meats; decent range of salads and tagliatelles, and an excellent selection of pastries and desserts; children's menu available. Evening gourmet menu is well regarded. ☎ +33 (0)4 79 41 13 11 ⓦ www.lesclochetons.fr.st

LA DAILLE

Boasting Val d'Isère's longest run means having to cater for those who need sustenance and a reviving cold drink on the descent. La Daille has a number of venues spaced out along the route, plus a number of venues easily accessible at the base area.

Les Marmottes € Nestled in the area between the Marmottes and Borsat Express chair-lift bases, close to the Snow Park. Reasonably attractive building with a piste-side terrace overlooking the chair lifts and views up the upper Bellevarde and La Daille sector pistes, as well as the public slalom stadium and a bit of the Snow Park. The terrace has a couple of drinks and snacks kiosks, plenty of deckchairs and picnic-style bench tables and seating.

  The interior is quite pleasant, with plenty of natural stone and wood; dining tables and seating are plain refectory-style benches; there's an open fire and a cute little ante-room perfect for small groups. Restaurant is self-service only, but has one of the best salad buffets on the mountain; other fare on offer is standard pasta and meat and vegetable centred.

La Folie Douce €€ Probably Val d'Isère's most enjoyable on-mountain bar and restaurant, accessible by everyone and with the resort's most rocking atmosphere. Every fair-weather day there are DJs with live music accompaniment on the huge sunny terrace giving the venue a buzzing ambience. La Folie shares the building with La Fruitière restaurant and the upper station of the Daille gondola; accessible by pedestrians and piste-side at the confluence point of the Verte, Diebold and OK runs.

  There is a drinks and waffles kiosk on the terrace, plus a basic bar counter for beer and shots. The large interior restaurant and

⬛ *And the beat goes on ... La Folie Douce bar and restaurant, La Daille*

bar is rustically decorated, with plenty of exposed wood and Alpine detailing, and has a smaller cosier mezzanine. The restaurant is self-service and offers the usual fare of pasta, chicken and chips, meat and vegetables. Hot drinks machines are also available.

La Fruitière €€+ Sharing the same building with La Folie Douce and the Daille gondola top station (accessible by pedestrians), this good-quality restaurant is unusually decorated to look like an old Savoyard dairy: tiled walls, milk churns and cheese-making accoutrements are matched with staff uniforms in the style of dairy workers. Booking is recommended at busy periods and the restaurant has a maître d' meet-and-greet service at its own private terrace overlooking that of La Folie Douce. The fairly wide à la carte menu is not adventurous, but the cuisine is of good quality and well presented; the wine list is excellent and includes a fair range of champagnes. ☎ +33 (0)4 79 06 07 17

Le Triffolet €€ An attractive modern chalet set in a clearing in the woods just above the final home runs to La Daille; accessible from the Verte, Diebold, OK and 'G' pistes. The main terrace overlooks the pistes and is easily reached from them. Pleasant interior dining saloon with full bar, double-height ceiling and an upper galleried dining area with a second terrace. The menu includes a good range of salads, tartiflette, pastas, steak and an excellent range of wood-fire oven pizzas. Set menu and specials too.

Les Tufs €€ Huge traditional chalet with rustic decor, conveniently sited at the foot of the Verte, Diebold and Orange pistes at La Daille beside the Funival station, with a large piste-side terrace accessible by all visitors. The terrace has its own snack kiosk plus table service and direct access to the large ground floor interior restaurant and separate bar, leading upstairs to a further dining room set aside for a good lunchtime self-service Savoyard buffet.

La Rosée Blanche €€ This is the small daytime terrace bar belonging to the evenings-only Le Barillon restaurant, situated a short stroll across the bridge near the Daille gondola. It offers a limited light bites menu, but is a convenient snack and drink stop if you are heading to or from the nearby ski bus stop.

La Daille's commercial centre €+ This backs on to the side of the pistes near the children's Snow Garden, by the huge Bellecôte apartments, and has a couple of bars and terrace restaurants offering reasonable-value snacks and set menus, mostly centred on simple pastas, grills and meat and vegetable dishes.

▶ *Snowshoeing off the beaten trail... reaching the parts that skiers can't!*

ALTERNATIVE ACTIVITIES

As befits Val d'Isère's position as one of the world's top winter-sports resorts, the station also promotes a wide range of other attractions to complement the main Alpine ski sports. Many are focused on high-adrenaline sports, but there are also plenty of gentler activities to appeal to all ages and abilities.

Full details and bookings are available via the tourist office.

❶ Activities may not be covered by travel insurance (see page 50).

SNOWSHOEING

This is the best way for non-skiers to get out on the snow and into the mountains. Modern snowshoes are made of lightweight materials and are easy to master. They work by spreading your weight over a wider surface area than normal, allowing you to walk more easily over deep snow, using a pair of ski poles for balance. Snowshoeing can take you far from the busy ski pistes and lifts and into more tranquil areas, where you may spot Alpine fauna such as the chamois, ibex, golden eagle and snow hare.

Way-marked itineraries are available alongside the cross-country ski circuits in the Manchet Valley and at l'Ouillette Lake near the summit of Solaise. There are also two wilder trails in the Fornet sector: following the route of the closed Col de l'Iseran road from Le Fornet further up the valley to the Pont St Charles near the Gorges de Malpasset, and on the crest of the Col de l'Iseran (the highest pass on the Route des Grandes Alpes) at the foot of the Pissaillas Glacier, reached by taking the Fornet cable car and Vallon de l'Iseran gondola (pedestrian pass required). Route details are printed on the reverse of the standard Val d'Isère piste map. Stay off to the sides of the pistes when in the ski zones. Equipment hire is available from all good Alpine ski-rental outlets at the resort.

LANGLAUF

Cross-country skiing (*ski du fond*) is not neglected in Val d'Isère. Dedicated Nordic circuits are located in four different sectors of the resort's ski area: routes and access details are printed on the reverse of the standard piste map. The routes are:

La Daille: gentle snowfields on the left of the main road towards Val d'Isère, just past La Daille's old village. The circuits are quite limited, but are not used much and are therefore ideal for nervous novices. However, snow conditions suffer quickly here at this low altitude and the area is frequently unusable. Green piste 1300 m (1422 yd) long; blue piste 2000 m (2188 yd) long.

Le Laisinant: attractive area in the snowfields and light woods on the opposite side of the main road from the hamlet of Le Laisinant, accessible using the Train Rouge ski bus. Access to the circuits is just across the road from the bus stop by the hamlet's upper road-side car park. Blue circuit 'Le Laisinant' 1300 m (1422 yd) long; red circuit 'Le Thovex' 3500 m (3829 yd) long.

Le Manchet: one of the best-established cross-country zones in the Espace Killy, with good mileage achievable amongst beautiful surroundings. It presents a genuine opportunity to get out into the more peaceful parts of the ski area, yet still within easy reach of major services. The circuits run along the floor of the Manchet Valley, starting at the end of town. The excellent Les Clochetons restaurant is at the start/finish area, and the Train Vert ski bus stop is in the car park opposite. Green circuit 'Les Chavonnes' 1400 m (1531 yd) long; blue circuit 'Le Gorret' 3000 m (3282 yd) long; red circuit 'Le Manchet' 6500 m (7111 yd) long.

L'Ouillette: Val's only high-altitude circuit, accessible via the Solaise cable car (pedestrian pass required), ensuring consistent snow conditions and with great views over the upper Alpine ski areas and peaks beyond. On arrival at the top of the Solaise, traverse the summit's Alpine pistes directly off the terrace of the Tête de Solaise restaurant, heading for the base of the Terrasse button lift, where there is an entrance to the circuit at this level. Alternatively, walk or skate over the crest of the summit straight ahead, veering right towards l'Ouillette restaurant, where the circuit begins immediately in front of the terrace on the shores of the frozen l'Ouillette Lake. One blue circuit 2000 m (2188 yd) long.

Langlauf equipment hire is available at all good Alpine ski-equipment rental outlets at the resort.

SNOW FUN

From 17.30 hours each weekday except Thursday, Val d'Isère's resort entertainment team are out on the ice rink and Front de Neige area. Events may include curling on the ice rink, football on the snow and toboggan trains down the beginners' slopes. Details from the tourist office. There's no need to book, simply turn up on the night. Open to all ages, but parents must accompany young children.

NON-SKIERS

A ski pass is not always required to participate in the alternative activities on offer, but you will need to purchase a pedestrian pass to use the ski lifts, only some of which are accessible to foot passengers (see page 63 for details).

MUSHING

This is a wonderful activity for all ages. Teams of husky and Samoyed dogs pull passengers in arctic sleds guided by an experienced musher through the more peaceful outskirts of the resort. Quick taster circuits and half- or full-day excursions are available, including trips out to the quieter nearby village ski station of Ste-Foy-en-Tarentaise. Mushing lessons are also offered to teach prospective mushers how to control the dogs and steer a sled on their own.

ICE SKATING

Val d'Isère has recently invested in a new outdoor ice rink, attractively landscaped to look like a small natural lake, in the buzzing Front de Neige area at the town's base slopes. The rink is open every day from 14.00–19.00 hours, and for floodlit skating until 22.00 one evening per week (currently Wednesday). It is easily reached by participants and spectators, being only a short, flat stroll from the town centre. Skate hire is available on site.

SNOWMOBILES & ICE-DRIVING

This is a fantastic opportunity to thrash a car, go-kart, snowmobile or quad-bike around a pisted circuit.

There are two permanent snowmobile circuits. One is at high altitude on the Tovière Plateau, based beside the get-on point for the Tommeuses chair lift above La Daille, and reachable via the Verte and Creux pistes or on foot via the Daille gondola. The other is at the Circuit de Glace ice-driving circuit near Le Crêt on the main road between La Daille and Val d'Isère. The latter also offers spike-tyre go-karts and quads, plus Alpine-driving lessons and is easily reachable by ski bus. Ⓦ www.circuitval.com

FLYING

The Alps are even more breathtaking when seen from a bird's-eye viewpoint. Helicopter sightseeing trips can be taken from the heliport near Le Crêt. Heli-skiing is banned in France, but you can arrange for drop-offs into nearby Italy. Transfers to and from airport and other resorts are also possible. Ⓦ www.saf-helico.com

Ultra Light Motorized aircraft flights are available from a specially prepared landing piste in front of the Bellevarde mountain restaurant at the top of the Rocher de Bellevarde, accessible using the Funival, l'Olympique cable car or Bellevarde/Loyes Express chair lifts. Credit card payments are accepted on site.
Ⓦ www.marine-air-sport.com

Alternatively, launch off the summit of the Solaise harnessed to a steerable paragliding canopy, in tandem with a professional pilot, for an incredible sensation of soaring silently above the slopes, with skiers far below your feet, before landing on the edge of the pistes in the valley for a real Bond moment.

◭ *Chocks away on Bellevarde*

SWIMMING POOL & GYMNASIUM

Val d'Isère's municipal swimming pool is situated beside l'Olympique cable-car station at the town base slopes. The pool measures 25 x 10 m and is set out with four lanes for swimming lengths. 🕐 Open every day except Saturday, from 14.00–19.00; late opening until 22.00 hours on Wednesdays.

Adult and child admission rates are available for either single entry or a 10-visit reduced-rate carnet; entrance is free for all holders of ski passes valid for seven days or more.

The complex also houses a Turkish bath and sauna, plus a well-equipped gym with specialist Alpine sports training machines and free weights (additional charge). Many of the larger hotels also have their own indoor or outdoor heated swimming pools and fitness facilities.

SPORTS CENTRE

Located just before the first tunnel on the road to Le Joseray, behind the swimming pool complex and adjacent to the Henri Oreiller Congress Centre. Facilities available include indoor five-a-side football, basketball, table tennis, volleyball, handball, badminton, trampolining, gymnastics and an artificial climbing wall. 🕐 Open every day 09.00–noon, and 15.00–19.00 hours
Ⓦ www.valsport.org

L'ADROIT FARM

An unusual opportunity to visit a real working Alpine dairy farm. On Mondays, Wednesdays, Fridays and Saturdays from 09.30 hours you can observe the cheese-making process. Daily guided tours from 17.30; cheese tasting and occasionally helping to milk the cows. Ⓦ www.fermedeladroit.com

APRÈS-SKI

Once the lifts close, the focus for fun turns away from the pistes towards the attractions of the resort and the social side of the snowsports experience. Val d'Isère attracts a cosmopolitan, sophisticated clientele and has the facilities to match, but it also has more than its fair share of good old-fashioned full-on party venues, with a legendary reputation for nightlife. Of course, there are also other less frantic distractions...

RETAIL THERAPY

Val d'Isère is a sizeable town with a year-round population, so its range of shops is reasonably extensive, although like at all snowsports resorts the majority of these are Alpine sports shops. There is a fair number of quality fashion boutiques, delicatessens, souvenir shops and several well-stocked large supermarkets. There are also a couple of pharmacies/perfumeries, specialist eyewear boutiques, newsagents, bookshops, an art gallery, photographic studios, video/DVD rental library, a florist's and even a tattoo parlour. Most shops and cafés are situated on the high street (avenue Olympique) and in the Val Village arcade. The town has four banks on the high street, all with 24-hour cash machines.

Monday is town market day. From early morning until early evening the high street and square in front of the post office are lined with visiting traders' stalls, some selling regional products.

Every Thursday evening the high street is closed to traffic from 18.00 to 20.00 hours and the resort centre is given over to pedestrians. Cauldrons of vin chaud are set out and the evening is animated by street entertainers and children's competitions.

◀ *Sundown at Val d'Isère, towards the Rocher du Charvet*

PAMPERING

Before Mediterranean beach holidays became popular, Alpine resorts were tourism's foremost destinations. Visitors came to rejuvenate in the clear, fresh mountain air and pursue 'wellness' activities and 'cures'. The trend is growing again and Val d'Isère now has a number of establishments offering a full range of health and beauty treatments to pamper or pummel you back to health.

After a day's exertion on the slopes, why not treat yourself to a massage or facial, lymphatic drainage or toning treatment, or a whirlpool, sauna or Turkish bath at one of the town's spas?

Thérapéos Balnéothérapie, in the Galerie du Thovex, place Jacques Mouflier (tourist office square).

🕿 +33 (0)4 79 41 96 77

Thermes du Christiania at the Hotel Christiania

🕿 +33 (0)4 79 06 02 90

Hotel les Barmes de l'Ours beauty suite available at hotel spa

🕿 +33 (0)4 79 41 37 00

CINEMA

Val has a two-screen cinema located on the high street. The films are generally in French or dubbed in French, although many are subtitled and there are frequent English-language screenings. See website for listings. 🆆 www.cinealpes.fr

SPECIAL EVENTS

For current details of all forthcoming events, major ski competitions and festivals, go to our website: **www.ski-ride.com**

RESTAURANTS

Val d'Isère has a plethora of eateries, many mediocre and most offering similar bland international fare, but there are a number of more committed and noteworthy serious restaurants as well. The following is a selection of the some of the best. Some are open at lunchtime; all are open for dinner 19.00–24.00 hours.

➔ *See Val d'Isère town plan on page 59.*

OUT OF TOWN

Le Barillon €€ Just next to the main ski bus stop in La Daille. Cosy chalet-style, family-run restaurant under the Rosée Blanche bar, with just a dozen tables. Specializing in raclettes, fondues, pierrades and tartiflette; vins du Savoy. On rough-weather days, the restaurant opens at lunchtime. ☎ +33 (0)4 79 06 12 09

Le Samovar €€ Pleasant Alpine-style restaurant at the family-run hotel of the same name in La Daille, located on the main road, facing the ski bus stop. Attentive and welcoming service, very good hors d'oeuvres and desserts buffet, plus a menu centred on Savoyard specialities. Wood-fire oven pizzas, too.
☎ +33 (0)4 79 06 13 51

La Vieille Maison €€+ A little oasis of charm in the otherwise austere surroundings of La Daille, situated in the middle of the old village, behind the Hotel le Samovar. This is a beautifully rustic old village farmhouse decorated with traditional farming implements and complete with a well. Serves an excellent range of starters, refined interpretations of regional main courses and a great selection of cheeses and desserts. Closed Sundays.
☎ +33 (0)4 79 06 11 76

Les Tufs €€ Another good La Daille venue. Big, buzzing, popular family restaurant housed in a huge Savoyard chalet at the foot of La Daille's home-run pistes, between the gondola and the Funival. Open wood-fire grill; Savoy specialities such as tartiflette, fondues and raclettes; good-value set menus and a good range of home-made ice creams. In the evenings, this is a short, flat stroll from all the main accommodation and main bus stop at La Daille. Closed Mondays. ☎ +33 (0)4 79 06 25 01

Le Chalet du Crêt €€€ Beautifully converted old farmhouse in the hamlet of Le Crêt, between La Daille and Val d'Isère. An excellent-quality restaurant with a gourmet reputation. Refined à la carte menu plus set menu options; short but select wine list. One of the area's most sophisticated venues. Closed Mondays. ☎ +33 (0)4 79 06 20 77 ⊕ www.chaletducret.com

La Becca €€+ In-house restaurant at the hotel of the same name in the hamlet of Le Laisinant, just up the valley from Val d'Isère. An attractive stone-built farmhouse conversion in a peaceful location; open central fireplace. Refined and adventurous set menu, with a select range of seafood and fine meats. ☎ +33 (0)4 79 06 09 48

Les Clochetons €€+ Attractive, large, new-built chalet, which is the last building in town at Le Châtelard. Accessible by the Green Line ski bus or from the Santons piste during the day; free shuttle bus service from Val d'Isère town centre in the evenings. Wide selection of fish, meats grilled on the open wood fire and well-regarded 'gourmet' set menus; excellent choice of desserts. ☎ +33 (0)4 79 41 13 11 ⊕ www.lesclochetons.fr.st

IN TOWN

Maison Chevallot €€ Not a restaurant, but an unmissable patisserie and café opposite the post office in the centre of the Val Village shopping area. Massive range of speciality breads, tarts and cakes, chocolates and ice cream, all elaborated in-house at this award-winning confectioners. 🕒 Opens 09.00 hours.
📞 +33 (0)4 79 06 02 42

Bar Jacques €+ Quaint little restaurant in rue Pigalle, near Dick's 'T' Bar. Ski instructor owner-run, intimate and welcoming. The menu has gourmet aspirations, but is very reasonably priced. Non-smoking throughout. 📞 +33 (0)4 79 06 03 89

Le 1789 €€ Tucked away up an uninspiring side alley, beside the Résidence/Gallerie les Cîmes on the lower main street, but an attractive venue all the same. Roaring log fire, Brazerade grill and wholesome Savoie specialities. 📞 +33 (0)479 06 17 89

Le Canyon €€ Front-line position on the lower main street, beside the Residence/Gallerie les Cîmes. Pierrades, fondues and raclettes, plus house speciality steak tartares; breakfast buffet from 08.00 hours at weekends and live music on Saturday evenings. Wine bar on lower ground floor. 📞 +33 (0)4 79 06 18 19
🌐 www.lecanyon.com

La Casserole €€+ Rustic, almost kitsch, two-storey cabin on the corner of the high street and rue Pigalle (leads to Dick's and Parking du Centre). Pierrades and fondues, open wood-fire grill; excellent aperitifs/digestifs selection and very good wine list; speciality ice creams. 📞 +33 (0)4 79 41 15 71

Les 3 Bises €€ Right next to/above Club 21 nightclub, so very handy for not wasting a minute. Popular and buzzing venue offering Brazerade grill, fondues, raclette and tartiflette; excellent-value set menu with wine and coffee included. It even has its own streetside late-night crêperie just in case you get the munchies while in the club. ☎ +33 (0)4 79 06 04 93

La Perdrix Blanche €€ Front-line position on the high street in the heart of town. Best known for its wide selection of fresh fish: lobster tank and sushi bar (Tuesdays only), but also pizzas and fajitas – around the world in 80 minutes! All-day service; good for afternoon cakes and coffee. ☎ +33 (0)4 79 06 12 09

La Luge €€ High street position under the Hotel Blizzard. Classy chalet-style decor and lovely aromas from the open wood-fire rotisserie. Savoyard specialities, including a range of speciality fondues; roast beef and lamb. ☎ +33 (0)4 79 06 69 39

La Grande Ourse €€€ Front-line position on the base of the town pistes, but accessible from the upper end of the street past the church. An old private chalet with an intimate ambiance, gourmet lunches and candlelight dinners; excellent selection of fish and select meat dishes; fine desserts and very good wine list. ☎ +33 (0)4 79 06 00 19

La Casa Scara €€+ Directly opposite the church in the old village centre. Nice venue specializing in dishes from the neighbouring Italian regions, as well as traditional classics such as saltimbocca and osso bucco; wide range of Italian wines. ☎ +33 (0)4 79 06 26 21

BARS & CLUBS

Val d'Isère still reigns as the French Alps' liveliest party capital, with a huge range of cafés, bars and music bars pulsing with activity from late afternoon to early morning. It has the usual selection of dives, but also a good number of bars that take the time to plan their weekly programme of themes and events, and make a real effort to stand out from the crowd. It is not cheap, though; expect to pay around €6 for a large beer, and €8 at late-night venues; cocktails will set you back upwards of €10. The following are some of the best venues (see town plan, page 59):

Bananas A Val institution, due to its great position at the lowest corner of the town's base slopes, making it one of the first ports of call for immediate après-ski. Patio heaters on the terrace help prolong the day; come night-time the downstairs bar is heaving and hot. Young crowd.

Saloon Another venue for those on an après-ski mission, tucked in behind and below the Hotel Brussels at the town's base area, reachable on-piste – they even have an attendant to mind your gear. Lethal cocktails.

Bar l'Alexandre Chilled hangout in the post office square, nearest the church. Snooker and pool tables; occasional Roots and reggae-themed evenings with DJ.

Morris Pub In-house bar at the hotel of the same name, just up the road towards Le Laisinant past the town centre. Has a rocking après-ski scene, with live bands; dancing encouraged. Massive range of flavoured vodkas.

Pacific Bang in the centre of town, underneath the big Precision shop. Big venue, big screen sports and a big weekly gear raffle. Popular with saisonnaires and chalet girls.

Le Petit Danois Tucked in up a back alley beside the restaurant La Casserole, just off the lower high street. English breakfasts by day, Scandinavian crowd at night – need we say more?

Warm Up Café Front-line position on the high street in the Alpina Lodge building. Cosmopolitan French ambiance, with sofas, cocktail bar, VIP bar and more mellow live music. A nice change from the Brit-heavy influence at most of the town's other venues.

La Forêt British tour operator-run bar at their chalet/hotel of the same name, up the hill from the lower high street. Rocking venue, with live bands, karaoke and decent happy-hour prices.

Club 21 Tucked behind and below the 3 Bises restaurant in the high street. One of the town's only true nightclubs. International crowd, international music policy. ◕ Open until 04.00 hours

Dick's 'T' Bar Last but far from least, the infamous Dick's. One of the best-known venues in the Alps, often imitated but never matched. Actually it is not that much to talk about, but the hype draws the crowds. The party starts, you check out the separate 'members' vodka bar; the music swings from House to Euro Dance to Cheese and back again, and before you know it... enough said! ◕ Free entrance before 23.00 hours; open until 04.00 hours

INTRODUCTION

Welcome to Moonbase Tignes, a buzzing metropolis beamed up to the realm of snow and ice in the High Tarentaise.

Architecturally, Tignes is not to everybody's taste. The resort was mostly constructed in the 1970s and visually it is still redolent of that age, although you may regard it as a retro classic!

When the ski station's designers first dreamt up the idea of plonking massive apartment blocks in this high-altitude wilderness, there were just two absolute prerequisites in their brief – easy access to some of the world's best skiing and guaranteed snow conditions. Indeed, Tignes pioneered the concept of ski-in, ski-out accommodation. The originally futuristic buildings may have dated, but the taste for skiing convenience has not waned.

Tignes boasts the highest and lowest skiable points of Espace Killy: La Grande Motte glacier at 3456 m (11,339 ft) and Les Brévières at 1550 m (5086 ft) – 1906 m (6254 ft) of vertical drop. Although it's not possible to ride non-stop top to bottom there are summit-to-base routes off La Grande Motte that deliver a continuous on-piste descent equivalent to dropping off Ben Nevis and diving 6 m (20 ft) under the Irish Sea – enough to keep any vertical junkie happy.

PRONUNCIATION

Tignes   Teen

Les Brévières   Lay~brev~ee~airs

Les Boisses   Lay~bo~aas

◄ *Val Claret and La Grande Motte across the Lac de Tignes*

The most emblematic image of Tignes' ski area is the towering massif of La Grande Motte. This ultra-high peak and its glacial permafrost allows the resort to roll out the white carpet earlier than any other major European ski station, opening in late September and staying open to early May. This truly is a station for all seasons, and high summer is no exception, with skiing on the glacier accessible during July and August, too.

It is a big, busy resort, with big scenery, but there's masses of acreage in the ski area to disperse the crowds, and the variety of terrain is huge: from the intoxicating altitude of La Grande Motte, to the long cruises down into the tree line at Les Brévières; and from the wild and peaceful off-piste at the Col des Ves, to the busier groomed motorways linking into the Val d'Isère domain from the Col de Fresse and Tovière.

Piste marking is much clearer here than in neighbouring Val d'Isère, with more regular directional signs and frequent junction markers making route-finding a lot easier than in the rest of the Espace Killy. Although there are a reasonable number of black runs on the piste map, most are fairly tame, but the area's Naturide ungroomed routes are an admirable feature. Thrill seekers look past the piste map, however, and see the real potential that this area offers for extreme off-piste, with some of the most serious and exposed routes in the Alps available if you have the bottle and the ability.

SOUL

Tignes is a lot more Gallic than Brit-centric Val d'Isère. French urbanites flock to the area every weekend and the resort works hard to animate the harsh surroundings of this high valley with regular events and entertainment; despite the austere facade, the town has a discernible soul. The town is split into two resort centres: Tignes-le-Lac and Val Claret, facing each other across the frozen lake in this high, treeless trough.

Tignes has another side to its character. Down in the valley below the resort there are two peaceful villages, which provide a more traditional Alpine experience. Les Boisses is a tiny hamlet perched above the huge dam at the Lac du Chevril, above the site of the original village of Tignes. A scattering of small hotels and a church are really all that the hamlet comprises, but it does have a chair lift linking to the Marais Plateau. It takes just one further lift from there to reach the pistes at the Aiguille Percée above Tignes. Plans are also afoot to build a gondola connecting directly to the same arrival point as Tignes' Chaudannes chair lift.

Les Brévières is slightly bigger, but has a collection of small hotels, chalets and restaurants clustered at the heart of the village for a more convivial ambiance. The village is dominated by the looming wall of the Tignes Barrage dam, but this is an attractive spot beside a small lake and has a welcoming atmosphere. The village is lift-linked to the Marais Plateau by gondola and to Les Boisses by chair lift. It also has no less than three home-run pistes, including the longest black run in the region – the Sache.

SUITABILITY

Tignes is not the best choice for beginners, although competent novices should find plenty to progress towards. The station is best suited to keen intermediates and advanced visitors craving big mileage and big vertical, and for those travelling early or late in the season and looking for peace of mind regarding snow reliability.

COMING & GOING

The only road to Tignes is the D87, off the D902 from Bourg-St-Maurice (30 km/19 miles). Bourg-St-Maurice can be reached by train (Eurostar, TGV or Thalys), or on the N90 road from Albertville (53 km/33 miles) via Moûtiers and Aime. Daily coach transfers are available from Bourg-St-Maurice and regularly from most regional airports. Further information: Ⓦ www.altibus.com
Ⓦ www.touriscar.net Ⓦ www.satobus-alps.com

By road: from Bourg-St-Maurice, the D902 passes through the village of Ste-Foy-en-Tarentaise and continues up the valley until the turn-off to the right for Les Brévières (2 km/1¼ miles). The open car parking at Les Brévières is free. The village is connected to the ski area by a gondola, plus a chair lift to Les Boisses village. Continuing on the D902, it is only a further 3 km (2 miles) to the next major junction point, the D87 turn-off for Tignes across the top of the impressive dam at the Lac du Chevril. The road also continues straight on for La Daille and Val d'Isère. Once across the dam, you arrive at Les Boisses. As with Les Brévières, the open car parking here is free. The D87 then climbs the final 6 km (3¾ miles) up to Tignes.

Arriving in Tignes, Le Lavachet is to your left, Les Almes to your right. Turn left at the petrol station to access the principal covered car parks and for Tignes-le-Lac Le Rosset and Le Lavachet.

The D87 continues straight on into a tunnel towards Val Claret; for Le Bec Rouge turn right before this into the side tunnel. Val Claret is a further 2 km (1¼ miles) through the main tunnel, via the lakeside road. At the first roundabout, turn left for Val Claret Centre and the covered parking area, or continue straight on for Val Claret Grande Motte; the entrance to the main open car park is immediately to the right.

TIGNES-LE-LAC TOWN PLAN

KEY

i	Tourist office	🚡	Ski pass sales point
🚠	Cable car	✗	Equipment hire shop
🚏	Bus stop	**P**	Parking
€	ATM cash machine	🛒	Supermarket
+	Medical centre	**+**	Pharmacy
✉	Post office	**†**	Church

HOTELS & APARTMENTS

1 Hotel Tignes 2100   **4** Hotel le Refuge
2 Hotel le Lévanna   **5** Village Montana
3 Hotel l'Arbina   **6** Hotel les Campanules

CAFÉS & RESTAURANTS (see pages 272–3)

1 La Côte de Boeuf   **3** La Montagne
2 Bagus Café   **4** Le Clin d'Oeil

BARS & CLUBS (see page 275)

1 Jack's Club   **3** The Red Lion
2 La Grotte du Yeti

To Les Boisses,
Bourg-St-Maurice

To Le Lavachet

Les Almes

3

5

6

P

Station

P

€

i

4

3

3

4

Promenade de Tovière

2

Le Rosset

2

Le Bec Rouge

Ice rink

Rue de la Poste

1

2

1

1

Aqua
Centre

N

To Val Claret

TIGNES

VAL CLARET TOWN PLAN

KEY

i	Tourist information	⬇	Ski pass sales point
🚠	Funicular	✂	Equipment hire shop
🚌	Bus stop	P	Parking
€	ATM cash machine	🛒	Supermarket
✚	Medical centre	✚	Pharmacy
✉	Post office	⬆⬇	Elevator

HOTELS & APARTMENTS

1 Club Med
2 Hotel le Diva
3 Hotel la Vanoise
4 Hotel Curling
5 L'Écrin
6 Hotel Nevada

RESTAURANTS (see page 274)

1 Auberge des 3 Oursons
2 Le Caveau
3 Le Grattalu
4 La Pignatta
5 Daffy's Café
6 L'Indochine

BARS & CLUBS (see page 276)

1 Fish Tank
2 Drop Zone Café
3 Grizzly's Bar
4 Le Melting Pot

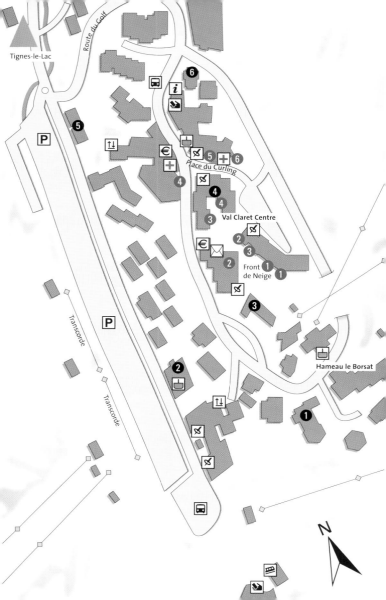

Tignes-le-Lac

Route du Golf

Place du Curling

Val Claret Centre

Front
de Neige

Transcorde

Transcorde

P

P

Hameau le Borsat

N

SKI AREA DATA

• Opening time	08.45 hours
• Last lift up	17.00 hours
• Skiable area	1200 ha (486 acres)
• Altitude	1550–3456 m (5086–11,339 ft)
• Vertical drop	1906 m (6254 ft)
• Access points	7
• Ski schools	20 +

• Ski lifts	90		
Cable cars	4	Funiculars	2
Gondolas	4	Declutchable chair lifts	19
Drag lifts	30	Non declutchable chair lifts	25
Rope tows	6	Free lifts	10
• Capacity	155,925 passengers/hour		

• Pistes	131 (= 300 km/186 miles)		
Green	20	Tricks parks	2
Red	35	Children's	4
Blue	60	Halfpipes	3
Black	16		
Nordic	44 km (27 ½ miles)		

• Hands-free ski pass	No
• Snowmaking	331 cannons
• First-aid posts	9
• Medical centres	5
• Mountain bars & restaurants	17 sites
• Visitor information	www.ski-tignes.net / www.tignes.net

Figures given are for the full Espace Killy domain.

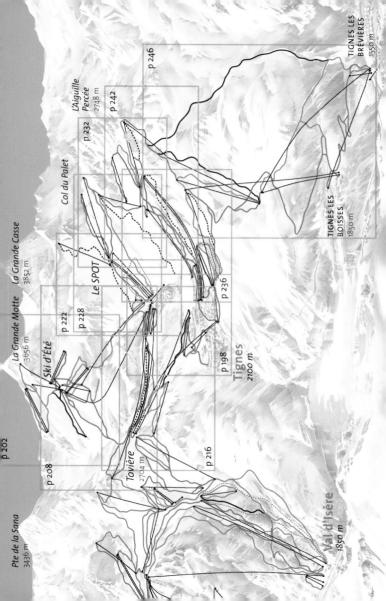

Pte de la Sana
3436 m

p 202

p 208

La Grande Motte
3656 m

La Grande Casse
3882 m

Ski d'Été

p 222

p 228

Le SPOT

Col du Palet

p 232

L'Aiguille
Percée
2748 m

p 242

p 246

Tovière
2704 m

p 216

p 198

Tignes
2100 m

p 236

Val d'Isère
1850 m

TIGNES-LES-
BOISSES
1850 m

TIGNES LES
BRÉVIÈRES
1550 m

SKI PASSES

Options available are either Super Tignes (covering all Tignes sectors, including the Tommeuses chair lift in upper La Daille), or full Espace Killy passes (also covering Val d'Isère, but only when the links are open). Prices are consistent throughout the season, with no high-season supplements.

All passes are available for children (5–12 years), adults (13–59 years) and seniors (60–74 years): half-day (mornings until noon; afternoons from 12.30 hours); full-day and multiples thereof up to seven days – the longer the duration, the cheaper the equivalent daily rate. All passes over seven days are for full Espace Killy.

Reduced-rate one-day extensions are available for all passes originally valid for six days or more. If you purchase a ski pass valid for two days or more after 15.30 hours on the preceding day, you can also ski that afternoon for free!

Ski passes are free of charge for all children under 5 years of age; from 5–12 years of age prices are approximately 25 per cent cheaper than adult passes. Ski passes for guests aged 60 to 74 years of age are approximately 15 per cent cheaper than standard adult passes; they are free for the over 75s.

Pedestrian passes for non-skiers are also available for certain lifts.

A photograph is required for all ski passes of more than one day's duration. The passes are not electronically readable and must be displayed at all times. Lost passes will not be replaced or refunded.

❶ Proof of age is required at the time of purchase for all child and senior ski passes.

❶ Accident insurance is not included in ski pass prices. Make sure you are adequately covered (see page 50).

SNOWSPACE SKI PASS

Another option for those on a budget and content staying in the Snow Park and the Palet and Brévières sectors, permitting access to these sectors only for about 20 per cent cheaper than the standard pass. Half-day and full-day options are available.

FREE LIFTS

There are several beginners' zones lifts that do not require a pass to use them, and are free of charge to all responsible users. These are the Pitots and Fil Neige drag lifts at Les Brévières; the Lavachet button lift in Le Lavachet; the Rosset chair lift in Tignes-le-lac; and the Claret button lift and Bollin chair lift in Val Claret.

SKI PASS SALES POINTS

There are six ski pass sales points in the Tignes domain:
Tignes Les Brévières At the base station for the Sache gondola.
Tignes Les Boisses Beside the post office in the church square.
Le Lavachet Next to the Sherpa supermarket (mornings only on weekdays).
Tignes-le-Lac At the Maison de Tignes-le-Lac.
Val Claret At the Val Claret Centre tourist office and beside the base station for the Grande Motte funicular.

Photo booths are available at all offices.

➔ See pages 181 and 183 for town plans.

PRICES
For current prices for all ski passes, tuition, childcare and other services, go to our website: **www.ski-ride.com**

SKI BUS

There are two lines operated by the ski bus service:

➔ **Line 1** Tignes Les Boisses **»** Tignes-le-Lac

➔ **Line 2** Tignes-le-Lac **»** Le Lavachet **»** Tignes-le-Lac **»** Val Claret

The line serving Les Boisses is a limited service operating twice an hour in the early mornings and afternoons. There are only two departures in the evening.

The main Tignes resorts service (Tignes-le-Lac–Val Claret) is an almost unique non-stop service, which runs continuously for 24 hours per day. The evening and night-time timetable is reduced to just two circuits per hour, but it is a great service all the same. In the evenings/night-time, the service also runs to Val Claret Centre, since this is where the majority of nightlife is centred. During the day, guests in Val Claret Centre have to take one of the pedestrian elevators down to the valley floor level to reach the main bus stop at the end of the road nearest the funicular base station.

The service is free of charge for all visitors; no ski pass required.

TIP

If you miss the last lift back from Val d'Isère or La Daille, there is a single link bus departing from Val d'Isère at 18.00 hours to return to Tignes-le-Lac and Val Claret only. The service departs from the main coach station in Val d'Isère. There is an additional charge for this service.

➔ *See page 59 for Val D'Isère town plan.*

EQUIPMENT

Most visitors travelling with a tour operator tend to leave the organization of equipment to their reps. Newly arrived guests are then usually taken en masse for gear fitting on their first morning, before going on the mountain.

Almost every sports shop in each Tignes suburb offers a snowsports equipment rental operation, so there is plenty of choice and competition to keep standards high and prices keen. All of the major franchises are represented, including Sport2000 and Twinner, InterSport and SkiSet, and there are also numerous smaller independent businesses, among them a good number of specialist snowboard shops.

All of the larger hire businesses also offer equipment servicing, waxing, edge and base preparation and repair services. The Snowtec workshop at Le Bec Rouge in Tignes-le-Lac is particularly well equipped, situated next to the post office.

NON-SKIERS

If you are a non-skier, but still wish to travel up to the mountain restaurants and viewpoints, you can purchase a 'pedestrian pass' permitting one round-trip on any of the four ski lifts that are accessible to pedestrians. These are the Sache gondola from Les Brévières; the Chaudannes chair lift and Aeroski gondola at Tignes-le-Lac; and the Grande Motte funicular.

Additionally, the Brévières chair lift from Les Brévières to Les Boisses and the Bollin chair lift at Val Claret are free of charge for pedestrians. Pedestrian passes are available for either one return journey on the funicular, or for a full day for all these lifts. Passes for child and senior age groups mirror those of the standard ski passes.

TUITION

There are well over 20 top-class ski schools in the Espace Killy, nine in the Tignes domain alone, so there is no lack of choice, with everything from standard group lessons for absolute beginners and progressing novices, up to advanced one-to-one teaching clinics for expert all-mountain riders.

The well-established French national ski school, the ESF, has six offices covering all Tignes' resort sectors except for Les Boisses. Ⓦ www.esf-tignes.com / www.esfvalclaret.com

There are also several specialized independent ski schools. The following are some of the best:

Evolution 2: ski and outdoor adventure tuition. Ski, snowboard, off-piste, Telemark, Nordic, heli-skiing, plus adventure activities such as ice-diving, paragliding and Arctic dog-sled mushing. Based at Tignes-le-Lac Le Bec Rouge and Val Claret.
Ⓦ www.evolution2.com

Snocool: specialist snowboard and freeride instructors and qualified mountain guides available for heli-skiing into nearby Italy; freeride trips into neighbouring Tarentaise stations and use of video and technical analysis. Based at Les Boisses, Tignes-le-Lac le Rosset and Val Claret. Ⓦ www.snocool.com

Kebra: founded in 1986 as the first dedicated snowboard school in France, but offering ski, Telemark and monoski too. Free beginners' snowboard lesson, plus equipment hire every Monday for the first 10 people registering after 17.00 hours on Saturday. Based in their own shop in Galerie Palafour at Le Bec Rouge.
ⓣ +33 (0)4 79 06 43 37

CHILDCARE

Les Marmottons Village d'Enfants has gentle Snow Gardens fenced off at the foot of the town slopes in both Tignes-le-Lac le Rosset and Val Claret. The one at Tignes-le-Lac le Rosset is the larger and by far the nicer of the two, within sight and easy reach of the resort centre and spread out along the shores of Tignes' frozen lake (which is barriered off).

The zones are equipped with magic carpet conveyors or rope tows, colourful obstacles and inflatables; specialist nursery ski instructors introduce children aged 3–8 years to the world of snowsports. The service is bookable for five or six consecutive half days or full days, either with or without lunch. Ski hire is not

🔺 *Starting out on the big adventure*

included, but can be arranged at an additional cost; equipment storage is available on site. The company also has its own restaurant and playroom equipped with TV and video. The staff speak French and English. Ⓦ www.marmottons-tignes.com

Ski schools offering childcare: Evolution 2 can also look after your children aged 3 years and above; the ESF accepts children from 4 years of age.

TIGNES

SERVICES

Medical centres: there are well-equipped trauma and X-ray suites available at two separate medical centres in Tignes: one at Le Bec Rouge at Tignes-le-Lac and the other at the main shopping area in Val Claret Centre. Neither are ski-to-door, but both are quickly accessible from the foot of the slopes in their respective sectors.

Cabinet Médical Tignes-le-Lac   ☏ +33 (0)4 79 06 50 07
Cabinet Médical Val Claret   ☏ +33 (0)4 79 06 59 64

The medical staff will contact your insurance company, but you will have to pay any initial costs, excluded by any excess clauses, on site. Make sure that your insurance covers heli-rescue, piste rescue and ambulance transport, as well as medical and hospital expenses. Tignes, along with Val D'Isère, has a network of on-piste first-aid posts dotted around the mid- and high-level ski area; all are permanently staffed by the piste patrol. There are two ambulance stations based down at Les Boisses.

Both Tignes-le-Lac and Val Claret Centre have centrally located pharmacies.

❶ Always carry ID and your insurance details. It is also advisable to carry a small first-aid kit for dealing with minor cuts and bruises (see Health & Safety, pages 46–50).

Telephones: phonecard and coin-operated public telephone booths are plentiful around the resorts' main streets and easily reachable from the base slopes. Once out in the mountains you will need to rely on your mobile if you carry one. GSM mobile phone coverage is virtually 100 per cent.

ATMs: in Tignes-le-Lac, cash machines are situated at the Maison de Tignes-le-Lac and at the bank on the corner of the big Bec Rouge building opposite it, as well as at the post office on the hill behind. In Val Claret Centre, there is an ATM at the post office at the Gallerie Commercial 'SEFCOTEL', a couple of hundred metres from the base of the Tufs chair lift, as well as in the arcade at the nearby place du Curling.

Mountain restaurants: there are half a dozen high-altitude eateries in the Tignes ski area that are directly accessible by lift and/or piste. All offer a full bar service, and most have snack food and self-service fare in canteen-style surroundings. A couple also have good à la carte restaurants offering more refined gastro-nomic menus and ambiance – reservations are recommended at busy periods.

➔ *See pages 259–62 for specific reviews.*

There are several more good venues over in the upper La Daille sector (see pages 154–6), reachable even with the Super Tignes ski pass. Tignes' town base areas also have a wide selection of venues easily accessible from the pistes, as does Les Brévières.

WCs: located at all Maison de Tignes tourist offices and at the Grande Motte funicular base station. All mountain restaurants also have public toilets; most are serviced and levy a small charge.

Shops: there is only one little souvenir kiosk at the Panoramic restaurant at the Grande Motte funicular upper station, but both town areas at Tignes have a plethora of retail outlets.

➔ *See pages 181–183 for town plans.*

SNOWFALL HISTORY & ANALYSIS

Although precipitation is unpredictable at very long range, patterns do emerge that are observable over a number of seasons. Using this data, you can tell if your preferred period of travel has historically seen good snow cover. The magic figure is 100 cm (39 in) – once snow depth exceeds this mark, conditions are generally good throughout the ski area and will remain so for a more extended period.

As is to be expected at this high altitude, Tignes is reliably snow-sure. The glacier ski area is open almost all year and the season begins earlier than nearly all of the other European mainstream resorts. Conditions stay strong thoughout the season, only starting to deteriorate in May; but increasingly predictable end-of-season dumps are always worth waiting for and the station is a local magnet when the other Tarentaise stations begin to suffer.

The chart below details combined averages recorded over three seasons immediately prior to the publication of this guide. Visit **www.ski-ride.com** for live snow reports.

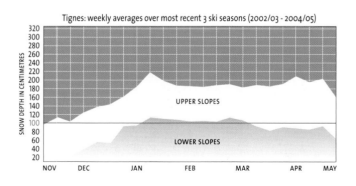

Tignes: weekly averages over most recent 3 ski seasons (2002/03 - 2004/05)

PREVIOUS SEASONS' SNOWFALL BREAKDOWN BY YEAR

The following charts detail the snowfall history for the three most recent seasons. Data from these charts was used to compile the combined averages chart on the preceding page.

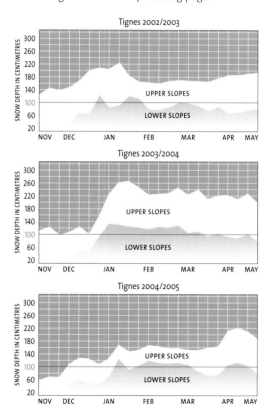

TIGNES BASE

Since Tignes is polarized into two distinct resort centres on opposite
sides of the lake, there is also a duplication of base areas and ski
area access points. Visitors based in either Tignes-le-Lac or Val
Claret have a choice of how they access their nearest slopes and
how they link with the other sectors; likewise with the beginners'
zones and end-of-day home runs.

Those staying in Les Boisses or Les Brévières have an easier
decision-making process since there is only one major lift up from
each village to link into the Tignes ski area.

TIGNES-LE-LAC

The main base focus here is the area right in front of the information
centre (the Maison de Tignes-le-Lac). It is wide and open, with
easy access to resort services and on-piste links to major lifts. The
quickest direct links are made via the Aeroski gondola. On arrival
at the top of Tovière you have the choice of crossing into the Val
d'Isère domain, making an on-piste link directly to Val Claret base,
or simply returning to Tignes-le-Lac, although this last option is
only possible via an advanced level piste.

On the opposite side of the base area are the twin Millonex
button lifts, serving the Gliss park and the lowest sections of the
home runs on this side of the resort, plus the twin Palafour chair
lifts that make onward links to the Palet and Brévières sectors.

From the side of the Maison de Tignes-le-Lac there is a pisted
track extending towards the lower Le Lavachet quarter, providing
a rideable link directly to the Chaudannes and Paquis chair lifts,
which link into the Brévières and the Tovière sectors respectively.

◀ *Front de Neige area at Val Claret Centre*

VAL CLARET

As in the case of Tignes-le-Lac, the disparate quarters of Val Claret are also linked via pisted tracks, permitting on-piste movement around the town. There are also two elevators accessible to slope users as well as to pedestrians. These link the lower town and upper Val Claret Centre commercial area.

The principal base zone is at the end of the main road, at the ski bus turning area, in front of the funicular base station and lift company headquarters. From here you can directly access La Grande Motte sector, the Snow Park and the Palet sector, and also link into the Val d'Isère domain using the Fresse chair lift.

A secondary nucleus of base services and lifts is located in the upper quarter of Val Claret Centre. From here the Tufs chair lift provides a direct link to the Tovière sector and towards Tignes-le-Lac and La Daille. This upper town centre is also the principal focus for the resort's shopping, bars and restaurants, and has a buzzing ambiance at the end of the day.

As the town stretches out in a linear fashion along the valley floor, a pair of long rope tows (the 'Transcorde') has been installed along the edge of the town's large, open car-parking area in order to save walking from one end to the other.

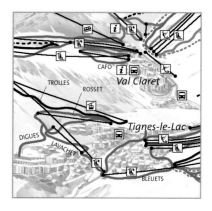

BEGINNERS' ZONES

In Tignes-le-Lac, the ski school meeting points are marked out in the gentle snowfields between the massive Bec Rouge buildings and the Aeroski gondola. The beginners' zone occupies the central base area nearest the promenade de Tovière, just in front of the Hotel Le Lévanna. The children's Snow Garden, playground and the resort's ice rink are also nearby on the shore of the lake. The area has its own non-declutchable four-person chair lift, the 'Rosset', with a wide and gentle blue piste of the same name running back down parallel beneath. From the top of this lift, there is also a piste traversing across to Le Lavachet (convenient for all visitors staying in that quarter of town), accessing another wide blue piste called Le Lavachet. This is served by its own gentle retractable reel-cord button lift, and is also reachable via the pisted link track running from beside the Maison de Tignes-le-Lac.

Val Claret's main ski school meeting points are in the Front de Neige area of Val Claret Centre, at the base area for the Tufs chair lift. The beginners' zone is, however, very limited here; it is served only by the one button lift, the Claret, which is quite steep and unsuitable for absolute beginners, as is the Cafo blue piste it serves.

The best area for beginners on this side of the lake is at the wide and gentle, but busy, base of the Prariond blue piste, which runs down to the Grande Motte funicular station and main ski bus stop in the lower town. The declutchable Bollin chair lift (shared mechanism with the Fresse lift, see page 212) serves the gentlest lower slopes, referred to as the Bollin blue piste, plus a quieter, easy green piste, called the Boïu, which is not marked on the piste map, but which runs parallel to the lower Prariond route, safely tucked away to the left-hand side of the busy main piste.

LA GRANDE MOTTE SKI SECTOR

This is Tignes' signature ski area, dominated by the peak of La Grande Motte itself, the highest lift-accessible point in the Espace Killy. This is a realm of rock, ice and permanent snow cover, as popular for skiing in July and August as it is in the winter months. Most people tend to focus on the glacier ski zone at the top of the mountain, but try not to miss the two summit-to-base routes. They deliver a truly non-stop on-piste descent of 1349 m (4426 ft). To reach the top from Val Claret base, lift access is by the quick Grande Motte funicular tube train or by two well-linked chair lifts, Les Lanches and the Vanoise.

LES LANCHES CHAIR LIFT

4

10 mins

- 748 m (2454 ft) vertical rise
- 2463 m (2694 yd) long
- 2400 passengers/hour

Given the ground that it covers, this is a fast lift and a good choice for those who get a bit claustrophobic using the funicular. The lift departs from the side of Le Carline restaurant at Val Claret base and journeys over the Double "M" home run from the glacier.

On arrival, the dismount point is right at the final lift pylon and cable-return mechanism, so be ready to leave the chair swiftly. You arrive directly on to the side of the shared Rimaye/Dahu piste, turning left to join them for the good, short link down to the Vanoise chair lift below left, or to continue past this for the Cairn blue and Double "M" red pistes. The Vanoise chair lift takes you onwards to the glacier area.

◀ *Summit of La Grande Motte*

VANOISE CHAIR LIFT

4¹/₄ mins

- 222 m (728 ft) vertical rise
- 1085 m (1187 yd) long
- 3000 passengers/hour

A good, fast lift serving the runs from the lower glacier area and providing an excellent link from Les Lanches chair lift to access the same 3032 m station area as the funicular. The chair is fitted with an automatic weather hood to give a more comfortable ride in this exposed high-altitude zone. The piste below is the Dahu red.

On arrival, the Panoramique restaurant and funicular station are immediately to your left, and the Grande Motte cable car is straight ahead; or you can U-turn to the right to take an access track around the far side of the restaurant to reach the Grand Plan, Face and Dahu reds, and the Rabotch and Génépy blues.

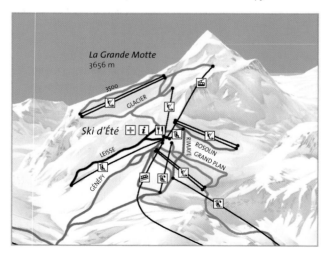

GRANDE MOTTE FUNICULAR

- 921 m (3022 ft) vertical rise
- 3450 m (3773 yd) long
- 3000 passengers/hour

167

7 mins

Officially named the Perce Neige funicular, this terrific piece of tube-train engineering whisks you straight up through the mountain from Val Claret base to emerge within the glacial zone. The base station is comfortably heated, with some seating, and has plenty of information screens detailing weather conditions, avalanche risk and indicating which pistes and lifts are open or closed. The platform is beyond a glass partition, which opens only after the train has come to a complete halt and descending passengers have cleared the area; this normally takes around three to four minutes. Once the doors open, it takes around two minutes' loading time before the train departs; board from either side. There is moulded seating up each side of the stepped carriages, plus hand rails for standing passengers. Never leave your gear against the sides or the hand rails – it will fall over.

On arrival, leave to either side and exit the station straight ahead on to the huge terrace of the Panoramique restaurant. A tool point and work bench are situated just to the right outside the station exit. Access to the pistes is straight ahead and to the right, around the rear of the restaurant building.

Another option is to disembark from the left of the train and leave via the automatic door to the side of the station. This exits straight on to a pisted access track, which gives a more immediate start to the Dahu red and the Génépy and Rabotch blue pistes.

The train is accessible to pedestrians and presents an unmissable opportunity for non-skiers to visit the glacial zone. Note that the last train down again is at 16.45 hours.

GRANDE MOTTE CABLE CAR

 6 mins

- 422 m (1385 ft) vertical rise
- 1640 m (1794 yd) long
- 1200 passengers/hour

Since this lift is the prime uplift for the glacier skiing area, queues can often build up, but the cabins are large enough to keep waiting time to a minimum. After the first couple of runs most people decide to range a bit further and use the alternative lifts.

Other than some exceptionally serious glacial off-piste, the cable car accesses only the one red glacier piste. Do not proceed unless you have the ability to tackle these conditions.

The views on the way up are terrific: La Grande Motte summit is directly ahead and the severe sheer face of La Grande Casse is ahead right. You are looking below over virtually the whole glacier ski area and, behind you, back down towards Tignes and to Mont Blanc on the horizon beyond.

On arrival, exit to the left off the platform to begin the Glacier red piste immediately.

CAUTION

You are now on a glacier, where dangerous crevasses are numerous even if you cannot see them. The Piste Patrol has clearly marked out the pistes and you are strongly advised to stay on them.

If you take off your skis or board, you become simply an unroped pedestrian in a serious mountaineering environment, so keep your gear on at all times when moving around on the glacier.

GLACIER & 3500

Who said glaciers were flat? The motorway-wide Glacier run has a mild-to-fair red gradient and, thanks to the extreme altitude and icy conditions, delivers a good, if somewhat bland, workout. The views are grandiose, extending over the whole Espace Killy. Val d'Isère's sectors are ahead right, against the backdrop of the Italian Alps; the Tignes domain is below left, with Mont Blanc on the horizon beyond.

Shortly after the uppermost section you can see the twin 3500 drag lifts rising up on your right-hand side. As well as linking with the Glacier piste they serve a shorter but similar profile piste (imaginatively called the 3500, too) running parallel on the far side of the lift-lines. The get-on points for these drag lifts are easily reached via a gentle pisted track on the lower right, before the Glacier run curves down left.

Another drag lift arrives on the left-hand side of the piste. This is the Champagny lift, which begins at the bottom left of the Glacier red piste and makes a fair link to the 3500 drag lifts to provide an alternative to the cable car for uplift on the glacier.

The onward descent is possible in two directions from the fast schuss finish on the Glacier piste. There is good signage at the junction point below, bang in the centre of the piste. Turn right for the Leisse black run, or left on to the gentler Rosolin blue piste extending out on to the lower glacier flow below (served by the twin Rosolin drag lifts rising back up to make a good link with the Champagny lift). Alternatively, veer left but keep high on the contour-line to head over to the Grand Plan and face red pistes, and/or to continue the full summit-to-base descent via the Rimaye blue link track; or simply stop and take the short Panoramic chair lift (two minutes) to reach the cable car and 3032 m services area.

LEISSE

This is only 750 m (820 yd) long, but often the best piste on the glacier, with a less icy surface and a direct fall-line descent. The entrance off the finish of the Glacier red, and from the 3032 m services area, is a gentle blue track, but the piste proper has a fair red profile and is frequently mogulled. The snowfields to the sides give a truer fair black descent, particularly when the moguls develop. This lower, more challenging side of the glacier is usually much quieter and is a bit more sheltered.

There is a good link to the Leisse chair lift on the bottom left. ⓘ Caution – this is still a glacier zone, so do not stray too far from the piste margins without a guide.

LEISSE CHAIR LIFT

6½ mins	• 263 m (863 ft) vertical rise • 785 m (859 yd) long • 2400 passengers/hour

This is the sole lift on this side of the glacier, making the connection back up to the 3032 m services areas and the cable car. There is a tool point at the get-on area.

The journey up affords good views up to La Grande Motte summit and over the Leisse piste, so you have time to study lines if you are going to stay and play in this quieter area of the glacier. On arrival, dismount to the right for the services area and funicular station (a track flows around the front of the terrace to access the Génépy and Rabotch blues and the Dahu red); the cable-car station is almost straight ahead. Alternatively, turn left for the flat access track over towards the Leisse black again, or to head to the Rosolin and Rimaye blues.

RIMAYE & ROSOLIN

The Rimaye is really just a link from the upper glacier to the Grand Plan and Face reds, and towards the Cairn blue and Double "M" red, to allow summit-to-base descents. The route begins between the Champagny drag lift and Panoramic chair lift. As well as being accessed from the Glacier red, this area also is reached via the gentle link track running between the Leisse chair-lift arrival point and the cable-car base station.

The Rosolin blue piste, running parallel to the twin Rosolin drag lifts, is over on the left as you begin, and it is easy to traverse over to join it. It is a short, straight blue, which allows competent novices to experience skiing in this high-altitude wilderness.

The Rimaye swings out higher to the right, picking up a fair gradient before becoming a contour-line track traversing across the top of the Grand Plan and Face reds, and cutting across the lines of the twin Double Plan drag lifts, to converge with the Dahu red.

⬥ Panorama from the 3032 m services area, La Grande Motte

THE FACE OF LA GRANDE MOTTE

Two flat and narrow pisted tracks run around each side of the
Panoramique restaurant and funicular station, emerging on
the far side of the buildings at a wide shared start area for a
number of routes on the face of La Grande Motte massif.

The twin Double Plan drag lifts arrive into this area on the left.
The pistes descending to the left of the lifts are the merged Face
and Grand Plan reds; the wide central piste on the face of the
mountain is the joint start of the Rabotch blue and Dahu red; and
the piste veering off to the far right is the Génépy blue.

The Dahu and Rabotch pistes split at a junction point about
30 m (98 ft) ahead after their shared start. The Dahu leaves to the
left, crossing under the line of the Vanoise chair lift, while the
Rabotch continues straight on down the face of the mountain.

The vistas ahead are stunning, with virtually all of Tignes
spread out below and an expansive range of major Alpine summits
on the horizon ahead, including Mont Blanc ahead left. All these
pistes can be linked to deliver a full home run to Val Claret base.

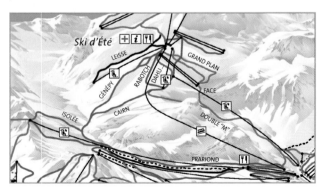

GRAND PLAN

The whole mountainside down the lines of the twin Double Plan drag lifts is fully pisted as a huge, homogenous glacial motorway. The gradient is fine, though, with a fair-to-good red profile on the upper sections. The Grand Plan and Face reds are the two marked routes here: the Face closest to the line of the lifts and the Grand Plan the line furthest out to the left.

The Grand Plan is a bland but fair red, swinging to the right at the bottom and merging with the Face red again to make a good link with the twin drag lifts.

DAHU

This piste shares its upper section with the Rabotch blue, then splits off to the left to descend almost parallel to the Double Plan drag lifts as a wide, good fall-line red, often with some moguls. It swings under the line of the Vanoise chair lift and directly down to link well with that lift below. Keeping high to the right above the lift gives access to the Cairn blue; or continuing past the lift begins the wide Double "M" red for the home run to Val Claret.

RABOTCH

After the gentle shared start with the Dahu red, the Rabotch continues as an enjoyable fall-line descent, with a fair red profile, directly down the face of the mountain to link with the Vanoise chair lift. Keeping high to the right above the chair lift, and continuing straight ahead, provides the best link to the true start of the Cairn blue, eventually joining the Génépy and Prariond blues for the home run to Val Claret.

CAIRN

This is accessed either directly from the Rabotch blue or via the gentle access track from the Rimaye blue, just beyond the Vanoise chair-lift get-on point. Both these gentle entrances and the blue designation belie the true nature of this short but enjoyable route. Cutting across the face of the mountain, towards the Leisse Valley, where it joins the Génépy piste, it certainly has a blue profile for much of the traverse, but the final section drops steeply on the flanks of the Rochers de la Petite Balme and is a real challenge for even early intermediates. The steep and deep freerides to either side of the final section are fantastic, particularly to the left, which is a very serious challenge.

GÉNÉPY

From the rear of the 3032 m funicular station and restaurant buildings, the Génépy flows gently over the glacial plateau and heads away from the hustle and bustle of the main ski area, entering a more peaceful realm of wide snowfields with views over the beautiful Leisse lakes valley below right.

After the initial green profile glide, the route develops into an enjoyable cruise, with occasional fast steeper sections. A mid-point junction simply splits the piste around a rocky outcrop (the left-hand line is the mellower of the two), and the two branches converge again a short distance ahead. There are plenty of deeper snowfields off to the sides, particularly to the left, before the Cairn blue joins steeply in from the left. The two pistes merge and schuss out on to the wide and gentle valley floor below. This last section is very mild, but has sufficient gradient to carry you through to the Prariond blue for the home run into Val Claret.

FACE / DOUBLE "M"

These really are La Grande Motte's signature routes, easily spliced with the uppermost Glacier red piste to deliver a true summit-to-base lung-buster. The top section of the piste shares the wide lower reaches of the glacier with the Grand Plan and Dahu reds, running parallel to the lines of the twin Double Plan drag lifts as a fast icy runway. This upper section can be played on using the drag lifts, or just keep on going below the lift queues and out to the right towards the line of Les Lanches chair lift.

The Face now forges its own route, away from the shared upper area and down on to the steepest pitch on the massif. The chair-lift pylon is bang in the middle of the piste; the route narrows considerably around it and is frequently choppy after heavy traffic. After passing under the lift-line, there is some serious steep and deep freeride off to the left (caution – cliffs to furthest left) to rejoin the piste below. The Face itself also swings down to the left, developing its most challenging profile to drop out on to the Double "M" below.

The motorway-wide Double "M" red actually begins at the end of the Rimaye blue at Les Lanches chair-lift arrival point further above. This wider, lower section is now mellower, although fast, but the stashes of deeper snow to the sides are the most inviting aspect. The edges of the piste are still demarcated with low snow walls like those on the glacier, rolled by the piste-bashers to mark the boundaries of the protected routes clearly, so unless you are lucky enough to spot a kicker to clear them, you will need to stop to step over them. The launch off into the wide river gully to the lower left promises the most fun.

The main Double "M" piste cruises straight down the line of Les Lanches chair lift directly towards Val Claret.

BOLLIN CHAIR LIFT

 3 mins

- 107 m (351 ft) vertical rise
- 570 m (623 yd) long
- 4000 passengers/hour

FRESSE CHAIR LIFT

11³/₄ mins

- 373 m (1224 ft) vertical rise
- 1585 m (1733 yd) long
- 2400 passengers/hour

This is an amazing piece of engineering, with two separate chair lifts sharing the same base station and travelling on the same cables by alternately filtering through the get-on area. Right-hand queue for the Bollin; left-hand queue for the Fresse.

The Bollin is one of the station's free-of-charge lifts, accessible to pedestrians, and is the one that should be used by novices – make sure you are in the correct queue. This lift is also useful for gaining height from the base of the Grande Motte and Palet sectors' slopes to link to the Tufs chair lift for the Tovière sector. On arrival at the 'mid-station', each alternate chair will declutch from the main cable and swing left for dismount directly on to the Bollin piste, which is really just the lower Prariond blue. Carefully traverse the piste to reach the Chalet du Bollin restaurant, or U-turn down to the left under the lift station for the track leading to the much quieter Boïu green piste.

The Fresse chair also declutches at the mid-station: remain seated, with the safety bar down. The journey resumes once the chairs reconnect with the main cable to continue up to the Col de Fresse. On arrival at the top, dismount straight ahead on to the flat col. U-turn right for the Isolée blue, or U-turn left for the Prariond blue; or go straight ahead veering left over the watershed to join the Col de Fresse green into the Val d'Isère domain.

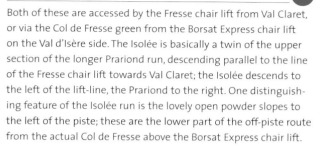

ISOLÉE & PRARIOND

Both of these are accessed by the Fresse chair lift from Val Claret, or via the Col de Fresse green from the Borsat Express chair lift on the Val d'Isère side. The Isolée is basically a twin of the upper section of the longer Prariond run, descending parallel to the line of the Fresse chair lift towards Val Claret; the Isolée descends to the left of the lift-line, the Prariond to the right. One distinguishing feature of the Isolée run is the lovely open powder slopes to the left of the piste; these are the lower part of the off-piste route from the actual Col de Fresse above the Borsat Express chair lift.

Both pistes have a mild red profile to start, running out to a milder and truer blue gradient at the valley below and joined from the left by the Génépy blue run from La Grande Motte. The Isolée ends at this point and all routes merge to continue as the Prariond. The torrent gully off to the left is a great playground for competent intermediates, with some nice natural kickers and rideable side walls, although the exit on to the Boïu green piste to finish is very flat.

The Prariond itself is a wide, gentle motorway blue, often busy and frequently chopped up at the end of the day. The major Piste "H" blue route from the Tovière sector joins from the right just above the piste-side Chalet du Bollin restaurant. Keep to the right-hand side, too, to take the Cafo blue track, at the next junction just above town, towards the good link with the Tufs chair lift, or just to reach the buzzing Front de Neige bars and restaurants area of the resort. The Prariond continues wide and straight towards the main base area, with good links to the Bollin/Fresse chair lifts, the Grande Motte funicular and Les Lanches chair lift. It is also just possible to skate over to the Balmes button lift for the Snow Park and Palet sector.

TOVIÈRE SKI SECTOR

This is the principal link sector for the Espace Killy, with a busy lifts junction and attractive mountain bar/restaurant at the summit of La Tovière, directly above Tignes-le-Lac le Rosset. Pedestrians can reach the summit using the Aeroski gondola too.

The shared Tovière pistes over in Val d'Isère's La Daille sector are covered in that section (see page 139), as is the fast Tommeuses chair lift serving them and linking back to Tignes.

The runs on the Tignes side make an excellent link across to Val Claret as well as directly down to Tignes-le-Lac, although the latter is possible only via a black run (novices can take the Aeroski gondola down to town to avoid it). From Val Claret, the link works in the opposite direction by taking the Tufs chair lift.

TUFS CHAIR LIFT

3 11¾ mins
- 560 m (1837 ft) vertical rise
- 1620 m (1772 yd) long
- 1500 passengers/hour

An older fixed chair lift, but still making a very useful link from Val Claret straight to La Tovière, for Tignes-le-Lac and La Daille. The lift departs from the busy Front de Neige area of Val Claret Centre, an easy stroll from the upper resort shopping street and accommodation. The journey up crosses over the Piste "H" blue run, linking back from Tovière, and gives great views over the rest of the Tignes ski domain. On arrival, the Aeroski gondola is almost parallel to the left. Turn right at this side of the restaurant for all routes except the Crêtes red, which begins straight ahead.

◀ *Pointe du Lavachet, Tovière sector, above Tignes-le-Lac*

AEROSKI GONDOLA

| 8½ mins ▲▼ | • 604 m (1982 ft) vertical rise
• 1804 m (1973 yd) long
• 3000 passengers/hour |

This is the key lift departing from the central base area at Tignes-le-Lac, accessible to pedestrians to access the high-altitude Tovière restaurant and providing uplift to the on-piste link to Val Claret and into La Daille for the Val d'Isère domain.

Just after starting the journey, look over towards the lake to see the freestyle ski practice-jumps, which launch jumpers into the lake in summer – come back in August to try it; it hardly hurts at all!

On arrival, the steps down off the lift platform bring you out on to a small, busy plateau. The Tovière restaurant is to the right and the Tommeuses chair lift is arriving ahead. There is a piste patrol cabin to the left, with first aid and tool point. The Crêtes red ridge run, towards the Combe Folle red and the Violettes blue pistes, is on the far side of the restaurant. All other routes are accessible via the pisted track on this near side of the building.

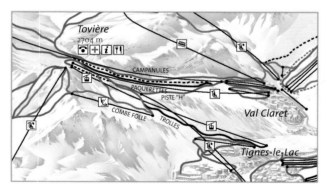

PISTE "H"

From the front of the Tovière restaurant, veer to the right-hand side of the wide shared piste flowing off the summit plateau, keeping high to the right above the clear route signs and piste map at the junction below: Piste "H" curves to the right over the watershed, continuing as a good broad blue.

After passing under the line of the Tufs chair lift the piste steepens considerably, with occasional moguls and fair red lines to the sides, down towards a wide junction area at the arrival level for the Paquis chair lift. Go to the right, past the arriving chair, to link to the Combe Folle button lift or for the Trolles black towards Tignes-le-Lac and the Brévières sector. Alternatively, keep left to remain on the Piste "H" towards Val Claret, La Grande Motte and the Palet sector. After this junction the Piste "H" continues as a fast undulating freeway, with occasional mild red pitches, more or less directly towards Val Claret; ending when it joins the Prariond piste at the junction just above the Chalet du Bollin restaurant.

CAMPANULES / ENVERS DE CAMPANULES

These are really just strong reds, but good long runs nevertheless. The Campanules is the pisted black, the Envers de Campanules is the ungroomed Naturide variation out to the left. Enter off the upper section of the Piste "H" blue, just after it passes under the line of the Tufs chair lift. Both routes are interesting cruises over the rolling terrain on this rocky flank of La Tovière, but they really only pick up a worthwhile gradient on the lower section above Val Claret, when they swing down to the right on the fall-line to rejoin the Piste "H" again; the final links to base and onward links are as per Piste "H" and Prariond.

PÂQUERETTES

This route was one of the first to be designated as a Naturide – part of an initiative by Tignes' piste management company to provide a safe environment for visitors thinking of moving on to freeride and off-piste. There are now six such itineraries in the Tignes domain, all tried and tested descents, marked out and avalanche protected, but always left unpisted so that users can have their first experience of 'off-piste' powder riding.

The descent is accessed via a narrow traverse around the back of the Aeroski arrival platform; the track is very flat, so boarders are best advised to walk. Once at the steep face, drop straight on the fall-line choosing any line you wish. The route exits on to the Trolles black piste below, for an easy link to the Combe Folle button lift, or to continue down to Tignes-le-Lac and Le Lavachet. Although it is short, this is one of this sectors' real gems for good intermediates and above.

COMBE FOLLE

This is accessed from the top of Tovière, via the Crêtes ridge run (see page 140), or using the steep Combe Folle button lift (no novices allowed) rising up parallel to the piste itself.

The descent is a very good red, with a direct fall-line profile, and is basically a pisted version of the Pâquerettes Naturide area running parallel beside it.

At the finish, at the base of the Combe Folle button lift, the only onward route apart from taking the lift is to continue the descent via the Trolles black piste straight down towards Tignes-le-Lac and Le Lavachet. To return to Tovière again take the Aeroski gondola from Tignes-le-Lac base.

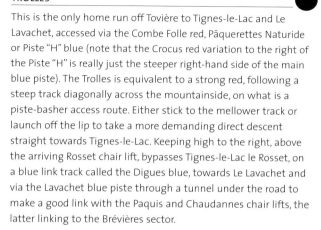

TROLLES

This is the only home run off Tovière to Tignes-le-Lac and Le Lavachet, accessed via the Combe Folle red, Pâquerettes Naturide or Piste "H" blue (note that the Crocus red variation to the right of the Piste "H" is really just the steeper right-hand side of the main blue piste). The Trolles is equivalent to a strong red, following a steep track diagonally across the mountainside, on what is a piste-basher access route. Either stick to the mellower track or launch off the lip to take a more demanding direct descent straight towards Tignes-le-Lac. Keeping high to the right, above the arriving Rosset chair lift, bypasses Tignes-le-Lac le Rosset, on a blue link track called the Digues blue, towards Le Lavachet and via the Lavachet blue piste through a tunnel under the road to make a good link with the Paquis and Chaudannes chair lifts, the latter linking to the Brévières sector.

PAQUIS CHAIR LIFT

 7 mins

- 442 m (1450 ft) vertical rise
- 1630 m (1783 yd) long
- 3000 passengers/hour

There are two chair lifts departing from this lower lifts junction below Le Lavachet: the Chaudannes to the left and the Paquis on the right. The Paquis rises up at a diagonal and under the line of the Aeroski gondola, arriving at a wide, flat saddle on the flanks of La Tovière, well below the summit. On arrival, U-turn to the right to link with the Combe Folle button lift towards La Daille (check on the way up that it is running), or for the Trolles black back towards Tignes-le-Lac; or go ahead right to join the Piste "H" for a good on-piste link towards Val Claret.

PALET SKI SECTOR

The Palet sector sits in the shadow of the neighbouring colossi of La Grande Motte and La Grande Casse. Although directly accessible from Val Claret and home to Tignes' innovative 'Le SPOT' freeride zone, Snow Park and competition courses, its lifts are a walk away from town, across the flat valley floor, and therefore it feels marginal to the rest of the ski area.

This sector has a greater potential than the piste map suggests, including the glorious off-piste routes from the Col des Ves and Rochers de la Grande Balme. The Col du Palet is also the starting point for an epic ski-touring route extending to the Paradiski ski domain (La Plagne and Les Arcs).

BASE LAYOUT

Val Claret is the furthest point reachable by car and the road terminates at the ski-bus turning circle near the funicular station. From here, and from all pistes running into this area, it is approximately a 100 m (109 yd) flat walk or skate over to the Palet sector's base lifts: the twin Balme button lifts and the Tichot chair lift. There is an electronic piste/lift information board, sector map and tool point at the base of the lifts.

The Snow Park is visible above town, on the hillside between the Double 'M' and Carline pistes. The base area is strung out in a linear fashion, with an open car park running parallel to the main road at the base of the competition slopes. A pair of long two-way rope tows ('Transcorde') runs along the edge of the car park. They do not link with any lifts but at least get you a little closer.

All home runs bring you to the area near the ski bus stop.

◀ *Skiing the Powder Of Tignes, Le SPOT*

TICHOT CHAIR LIFT

4

9¼ mins

- 363 m (1191 ft) vertical rise
- 1194 m (1306 yd) long
- 2200 passengers/hour

This is a slow, old chair lift, but it makes a good liaison with all onward lifts into the Palet sector and for the circuitous link towards Tignes-le-Lac and l'Aiguille Percée sector, as well as towards the Snow Park. The journey up gives an impressive view to the far left, up the line of the Col des Ves chair lift towards the sombre face of the Aiguille Noire de Pramacou and the monstrous wall of La Grande Casse behind.

On arrival, leave to the left to begin the Carline blue piste immediately. A little further down on the left is the arrival point for the Balme button lifts.

Keep to the right to reach the Palet restaurant, and to run around to the front of the terrace for a fair link with the Grattalu chair lift and Col du Palet button lift – take care when approach-

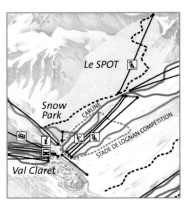

ing this area because pistes are joining from above right. Alternatively, stay central to descend a bit further for a good link with the Col des Ves chair lift, or simply to continue the descent on the Carline blue piste, swinging down to the left towards the Snow Park, Stade de Slalom red and Val Claret base.

BALMES BUTTON LIFTS

  5³/₄ mins

- 344 m (1129 ft) vertical rise
- 1160 m (1269 yd) long
- 600 passengers/hour x 2
- Difficult lift
- No beginners

These are a pair of button lifts, which run parallel to the Tichot chair lift, arriving at a very similar height, with the same onward options, but in a much quicker time than the chair lift.

On arrival, turn left on to the upper Carline blue piste, or U-turn down the line of the lifts for the steepest lines towards the competition course pistes.

CARLINE

This is a vast well-groomed blue starting at the top of the Balmes button lifts and Tichot chair lift, and running down to the wide confluence area at the Palet restaurant. It gives fair links to the Grattalu, Col du Palet and Col des Ves lifts, and is joined by the Grattalu and Signal pistes for the onward descent to Val Claret.

Heading towards base, past the Col des Ves chair lift, there is a junction point ahead: veer left for the fast Stade de Slalom red competition course, running parallel to the lines of the Balmes button lifts, or veer to the right for the easiest route towards Val Claret and the entrance into the Snow Park. The Carline stays central and runs straight down to Val Claret as a wide, mild red, eventually schussing out into the base area below. At the finish, turn sharp left to reach the Balmes and Tichot lifts, or keep going ahead towards the ski bus stop (ahead left) or the Les Lanches chair lift (ahead right) towards La Grande Motte. All other lifts can be reached only by walking. Check your speed in this busy finish area and keep an eye for fast traffic from above right.

SNOW PARK

During the summer months, Tignes has one of the largest glacier Snow Parks in Europe; the Snow Park signs you occasionally see on La Grande Motte are for that, so ignore them because it is not there in the winter. The winter park does not really compete on the European scene nearly as well, being quite a compact area with a limited range of modules. However, it is just above Val Claret and therefore easy to reach first thing in the morning and, combined with the 'Backcountry Freestyle' zone in Le SPOT, it certainly provides a respectable facility.

If you are content playing in this sector and l'Aiguille Percée sector, then go for the Snowspace ski pass (see page 187), which will save you about 20 per cent compared to the full area pass.

The park occupies the area on the lowest flanks of the Rochers de la Grande Balme, with a vertical drop of around 120 m (394 ft). It is equipped with a rope tow, although this really only serves the principal halfpipe.

Modules

Full-on halfpipe 120 m (394 ft) long.
Novices halfpipe 70 m (230 ft) long.
Various kickers Sizes depending on snow cover.
Rails Including S-rails, C-rails and a selection of flat/flat-down rails.

The park also has a 'Beach Zone' chillout area near the base of the rope tow.

🔺 *Pipe action, Tignes Snow Park*

Le SPOT

Tignes was one of the pioneers of the 'Naturide' concept, whereby popular freeride descents between the pistes are secured and trail-marked by the piste patrol team, but left unpisted as natural powder fields. The initiative is designed to allow good intermediates to progress towards off-piste and freeriding, within the relative safety of the patrolled ski area.

Le SPOT (acronym for Skiing the Powder Of Tignes) is the latest development of the idea and is marketed as the first facility of its type in France. The area is clearly marked on the upper right of the piste map, in the wild and peaceful side valley below the brooding Aiguille Noire de Pramecou, and is served by the Col des Ves chair lift and Col du Palet button lift. An information cabin is based near the Palet restaurant, with specialist members of the piste patrol on hand all day to answer questions about snow conditions, avalanche risk and weather forecasts. The team's principal objective is to educate visitors on the correct procedures and equipment necessary for safer freeriding. To this end they offer detailed explanations of the avalanche risk-level charts, instructions on how to read the general and localized risk bulletins, why and how avalanches happen and how to decode the detailed weather synoptic. They also have a display of photographs of Le SPOT's freeride areas as they look in summer, showing all the rocks and gullies that lie beneath winter's blanket of snow, and helping you to avoid hidden dangers and learn where and why cornices and wind lips form. This is a great opportunity to chat with ski-station professionals and get the best possible start to your freeride aspirations.

Detailed information leaflets are available from the Maison de Tignes and Le SPOT information cabin.

Le SPOT has 6 distinct zones:

ARVA® training Acronym for Appareil de Recherche des Victimes d'Avalanche – equipment for finding avalanche victims. Avalanche rescue transmitters are indispensable kit for anyone participating in off-piste and back-country touring, and this training zone lies at the heart of the area, both physically and philosophically. Eight transmitters have been buried in the snowfields between the Col des Ves and Col du Palet lifts, fanning out from the information cabin. The information team demonstrate how to use the avalanche search equipment and you can practise using the gear to locate the randomly programmed transmitters.

Naturide The Col des Ves route used to be the main black piste in this area; now it is left ungroomed. The route begins steeply, immediately to the left on arrival from the Col des Ves chair lift, but the rest of the descent is equivalent to a decent red, with quite a gentle mid-section before running to the base of the Col des Ves chair lift again (fair links to the Col du Palet button lift and Grattalu chair lift are also possible). Keeping high to the right and bypassing the lifts level takes you towards the Snow Park.

Softride This freeride zone is the powder bowl out to the right as you arrive on the Col des Ves chair lift, descending to the left of the lift-line to join the Col des Ves Naturide route. The area is promoted as a 'soft' introduction to freeriding, with the gentlest gradients being located in this area and plenty of open space to start developing your powder technique.

Hardride A more serious freeride zone on the steep upper flanks of the Rochers de la Grande Balme, descending wide to the right of the Col des Ves lift-line. This is a classic freeride for advanced skiers and boarders, with gnarly terrain and steep drop-offs. Go in tooled up.

Backcountry Freestyle This is the unpisted area immediately above the Snow Park and provides a great run-in to the park. The angle of the slope is perfect for building cheese-wedge kickers to augment the natural bumps and rollers and design your own modules to extend the park below.

Border/Skier Cross A permanent course set up on the Signal blue piste off the top of the Col du Palet button lift, which departs from in front of the Palet restaurant. The course is well maintained, with around seven banked turns and a series of jumps, rollers and compressions. Run-out is to the Palet restaurant area again, with good links to the Col du Palet, Grattalu and Col des Ves lifts, or onwards to Val Claret base via the Carline piste and/or the Snow Park. The Col du Palet button lift serving the run has a vertical rise of 266 m (873 ft) and takes 6½ minutes.

COL DES VES CHAIR LIFT

15¼ mins
- 422 m (1385 ft) vertical rise
- 2050 m (2243 yd) long
- 1350 passengers/hour

This is reserved for experienced skiers and snowboarders only, serving Le SPOT's Col des Ves Naturide route and Softride/Hardride freeride zones. There is a tool point at the operator's hut at the get-on area.

The slow journey up gives time to check out the lie of the land and plan lines over the open freeride areas descending on either side of the lift-line. On arrival, dismount to the right for the Softride zone, or turn left for the Col des Ves Naturide and Hardride zone. The lift operator's hut here is equipped as a first-aid post and serves as an information point.

GRATTALU CHAIR LIFT

6	4½ mins	• 315 m (1034 ft) vertical rise
		• 3000 passengers/hour

This is a fast six-seater, inaugurated during the 2004/05 season to enhance the link from the Palet sector towards Tignes-le-Lac and l'Aiguille Percée, as well as serving the eponymous wide blue motorway that runs to the right. The lift departs from in front of the Palet restaurant, next to the Col du Palet button lift. The journey up has great views to the left over the Col des Ves/Le SPOT.

On arrival, turn right to start the Grattalu and Lac blue pistes immediately. There is a ski-patrol information/first-aid cabin over to the far side of the piste. Another option for more experienced riders is to leave to the left and drop in to the wide open freeride that leads over towards the Signal blue and Boarder/Skier Cross area; it is a nice area for a picnic, too.

This vantage point also affords a grandiose view over the Col du Palet and towards the summit of Bellecôte on the horizon, marking the top of La Plagne's ski area.

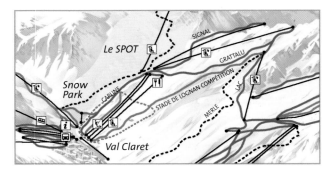

GRATTALU

A broad, well-groomed runway with occasional mild red pitches, directly from the top of the Grattalu chair lift back down to the Palet restaurant area. After the uppermost section, keep to the right; the first split to the left is for the Lac blue piste linking towards Tignes-le-Lac and l'Aiguille Percée sector, just above the arrival level of the Merles chair lift. This next section of the Grattalu is also shared by the Stade de Lognan-Compétition red, which runs parallel to the left before continuing on a more direct fall-line towards Val Claret; keep to the right for the Grattalu.

STADE DE LOGNAN-COMPÉTITION

This wide red shares the mountainside with the Grattalu blue. Officially beginning at the arrival level for the Merles chair lift, it slices down the fall-line as a good, fast, mellow red and is Tignes' Giant Slalom competition course.

Just after the Grattalu departs, the course picks up a steeper gradient and flows fast off the shoulder of the mountainside for the final steeper section down into the finish stadium. Keep to the right at the finish to make the best possible link with the Tichot chair lift; all other lifts require a hike.

⬥ *Competition course finish area*

MERLE

Another of the Tignes Naturides, accessible using the Grattalu or Merles chair lifts. Starting from the arrival level of the Merles lift, take the direct fall-line between the Lac and Stade de Lognan-Compétition pistes, for a good red equivalent gradient. This top section gets tracked out quite quickly, as traffic on the neighbouring pistes wanders off the sides into the inviting powder field. However, once you begin to leave the proximity of the pisted runs, the route takes on its truer freeride characteristics.

The route swings left towards the Merles chair lift, to proceed safely past the hidden, but roped off, rocky outcrops and cliffs ahead, and ride towards the depression in the terrain below left. This is the start of a lovely, steep, wide couloir funnelling out into the more open Lognan slopes below.

As this side of the valley is fully exposed to the sun for most of the day, the slopes here are highly prone to slippage and the piste patrol may close this lower section. If this happens, just take the Merles lift, or slog over to the Grand Huit or Replat lifts visible across the flat Chardonnet lakes area. Otherwise, the next bit is the best bit!

The couloir forces short turns and a direct fall-line descent to run out on to the open slopes beyond, with plenty of opportunity to leap off wind-blown kickers and boulder drop-offs to the sides. The Lognan slopes below are wide and frequently very heavy in the afternoon, but it is an enjoyable descent, with a great view ahead towards the lake, resort conurbations and the Tovière sector opposite. Aim for the cluster of chalets by the lakeside nearest Val Claret, keeping your eyes peeled for the ski bus stop. The finish is by the lakeside road, well away from any lifts, so you'll have to catch the bus back to town.

LAC

The sole link piste between the Palet and l'Aiguille Percée sectors, descending from the top of the Grattalu chair lift alongside the Grattalu blue piste, then past the arrival point of the Merles chair lift and to the left of the Merles Naturide and Stade de Lognan-Compétition red. This section shares the same terrain and gradient as these other routes, but runs closer to the rocky flanks of the Pointe du Chardonnet, which thrusts above left. Its menacing chutes and couloirs are well protected with Gasex avalanche dispersal blast-pipes, visibly sticking out of the rocky slopes above.

The route is then a very good blue, bordering on red, particularly if you keep high left to flow off the shoulder of the hill for the steep variation route towards a good link with the Grand Huit chair lift below left. Continue straight on and curve down to the left to reach the Merles chair lift – take care on the final approach because the piste narrows considerably into a compression dip. The piste map also shows a link straight ahead to the short Replat button lift, for a seemingly more direct route towards Tignes-le-Lac, but since this is on the far side of this absolutely flat Chardonnet plateau, it is best to take the chair lifts to gain height and to give more options for onward routes.

🔺 *The wild and rugged Palet sector, viewed from l'Aiguille Percée*

MERLES CHAIR LIFT

5³/₄ mins

- 260 m (853 ft) vertical rise
- 3000 passengers/hour

Another recent, and long overdue, upgrade to the lifts on this side of the valley, making a good link between l'Aiguille Percée and Palet sectors. The reason why the lift is quite a way across this flat plateau, if you are approaching via the Lys/Bruyères blue pistes from l'Aiguille Percée, is that there are two tarns in this area during the summer, and the nearest solid ground is where the lift has been sited.

The journey up gives a clear view up to l'Aiguille Percée rock formation on the skyline on the far right. Travelling over the get-on point for the Grand Huit chair lift and up the rocky flanks of the Pointe du Chardonnet, keep an eye out for the Gasex avalanche blast-pipes sticking out of the rocky couloirs above right. On arrival, turn left for all routes: the Grattalu and Lac blues; Merle Naturide black and Stade de Lognan-Compétition red.

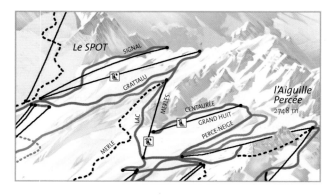

GRANDE HUIT CHAIR LIFT

7¼ mins

- 230 m (755 ft) vertical rise
- 852 m (932 yd) long
- 2400 passengers/hour

On the piste map it appears that this lift is out on its own and only reachable by the Centaurée blue piste. However, on the ground, the Lac piste provides a very good link (see page 231). If you miss the last lift up, you can also skate across this flat plateau to exit via the Anémone/Gentiane blue pistes towards Tignes-le-Lac, but these are a real flat slog to reach.

The journey up gives you time to appreciate this quieter, wilder region, with great views up to the Aiguille du Chardonnet above left, and l'Aiguille Percée above right; the wall of the arête ahead shelters this secluded cirque.

On arrival, turn left for the gentle sweeping Centaurée blue, the entire route of which is visible to the left on the journey up; or turn right for the Perce-neige blue and Ancolie red towards the Aiguille Percée chair lift and onward links to leave the Palet sector.

PERCE-NEIGE

From the Grand Huit chair lift, this route makes the link into l'Aiguille Percée sector and towards Tignes-le-Lac. Approximately 70 m (230 ft) from the top, there is a junction to the left; this is the start of the Ancolie red variation. The Ancolie keeps highest to the left, flowing off the shoulder of the hill for the fastest and best link to the Aiguille Percée chair lift. The Perce-Neige blue continues straight down as a wide standard blue, sweeping round the contour-line to the lower left for a final flat schuss to the Aiguille Percée chair lift.

L'AIGUILLE PERCÉE SKI SECTOR

This offers some of the most varied terrain in the Tignes domain – from the eponymous 'Pierced Needle' rock formation at the picturesque summit of this sector, to the long and forested slopes descending all the way to the lowest skiable reaches of the Espace Killy, at the traditional hamlets of Tignes les Boisses and Tignes les Brévières. It includes long blue excursions for competent novices, a handful of good cruising reds for intermediates, and a truly epic summit-to-base black with a 1156 m (3793 ft) vertical drop.

BASE LAYOUT

This sector is easily the most accessible from the central resort: the main cluster of lifts is immediately to the left of the huge Maison de Tignes-le-Lac information centre, with a number of home-run pistes flowing into this area. The pisted link track departing through the right-hand arch of the information centre can be used to ride down to the base of the major Chaudannes chair lift, via the tunnel under the road from Le Lavachet, tucked down beside the Tovière sector's Paquis chair lift. Alternatively, simply walk around the far side of the Maison de Tignes-le-Lac to reach the Millonex, Palafour and Almes lifts.

If you are staying in the upper Le Bec Rouge area, and are at least a competent intermediate, then you also have the option of taking the steep Chardonnet button lift from the roadside above town. This provides uplift to join the Anémone, Gentiane and Combe blues. On the piste map it also appears to make a link with the Merles chair lift into the Palet sector, but in practice this is a bit of a slog.

◀ L'Aiguille Percée (the Pierced Needle). See page 243

CHAUDANNES CHAIR LIFT

5 mins

- 388 m (1273 ft) vertical rise
- 1203 m (1316 yd) long
- 3000 passengers/hour

The Chaudannes shares its get-on area with the Tovière sector's
Paquis chair lift. There is a piste map, electronic information board
and tool point in front of the two side-by-side chair lifts: the
Paquis rises to the right, the Chaudannes to the left. This fast lift
makes the liaison towards the Brévières side of the sector, arriving
at the same altitude as l'Alpage/Lo Soli restaurant; the lift is
accessible to pedestrians.

The journey up travels over the main road, rising up the quiet
south-eastern flanks of l'Aiguille Percée, under the impressive
russet rock pinnacles that tower above this area – keep an eye out
for marmottes on the untracked slopes below. The views over your
left shoulder are across the entire Tignes domain.

The lift arrives at the side of the restaurant: swing left for easy
access to the terrace or to reach the Bleuets red piste; or
dismount straight ahead on to this wide, gentle, confluence area,
veering right
for all other
directions via the
Rhododendron
blue piste. The
piste flowing
towards you into
this area is the
Corniche run
from the top of
l'Aiguille Percée.

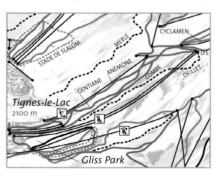

MILLONEX BUTTON LIFTS

1¹⁄₄ mins

- 61m (200 ft) vertical rise
- 244 m (267 yd) long
- 600 passengers/hour x 2

A twin pair of button lifts running parallel up from the base to serve the short slopes directly above town; designated as the Gliss Park tricks zone. These lifts are also handy for anyone staying in Le Bec Rouge or Les Almes areas of town, because you can use them to gain height to ride over to the upper parts of town.

GLISS PARK

This area immediately above the resort, running down to the Maison de Tignes-le-Lac, used to be the main Tignes Snow Park. Now that this has moved to its new base up at Val Claret, the zone is maintained as a secondary park and is ideal for novice riders. Modules normally include some banked turns, a head-to-head slalom and kiddies' fun trail. The area is further animated with urban music played over the PA system.

This area is also frequently used to host fun events, such as the end-of-season 'splash' contest where competitors schuss towards a specially constructed pool and attempt to water-ski across it!

> **MILLONEX SKI PASS**
> Enquire at the ski pass offices about this great deal, which permits access solely to the twin Millonex button lifts for a single-figure price – allowing you to use the Gliss Park all day. Perfect for youngsters and those on tight budgets. At certain periods, these are also free!

ALMES BUTTON LIFT

2³/4 mins	• 187 m (614 ft) vertical rise • 597 m (653 yd) long • 900 passengers/hour

This is another short button lift rising from the town level, just above the roadside nearest the suburb of Les Almes. It serves the slalom competition course and the cluster of short pistes parallel to it. It is also useful for gaining height from this side of town to make it easier to reach the major lifts.

The lift serves no less than three piste-mapped runs. However, in practice these all share a similar profile and are in effect the finish sections of the home runs returning from the top of the Chaudannes chair lift.

Primevères Black, U-turn to the left on arrival; a standard red that takes the steepest line down the right-hand side of the lift-line.

Colchiques Red, U-turn to the right on arrival; a mellower twin of the Primevères.

Stade de Slalom Blue, turn right on arrival, taking the widest and mildest line out to the left of the lift-line and merging with the end of the major home runs. This option also connects well with the Bleuets blue link-track that runs above Les Almes and down under a short tunnel beneath the main road to make a good link with the Chaudannes and Paquis chair lifts.

▲ *Tignes-le-Lac base station*

PALAFOUR CHAIR LIFTS

| 10 mins | • 474 m (1555 ft) vertical rise
• 1332 m (1457 yd) long
• 1700 passengers/hour x 2 |

Other than the Chaudannes chair lift from the lower part of town, these twin fixed chair lifts are the prime link from base into this sector. They are based just beyond the left-hand arch at the side of the Maison de Tignes-le-Lac and rise over the Gliss Park to arrive at the Aire de Palafour above the Beau Plan and Chardonnet lakes plateaux. They give superb vistas over the whole Tignes domain to the left on the journey up and, nearing the top, a great view of l'Aiguille Percée rock formation above right.

On arrival, dismount straight ahead on to the wide, gentle sub-summit, which has a piste map and directional signage. Turn right for the Oeillet Naturide; veer left for the Lys and Anémone blues.

OEILLET

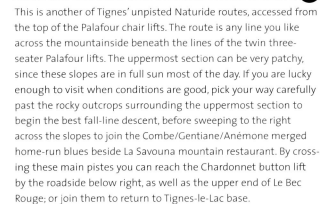

This is another of Tignes' unpisted Naturide routes, accessed from the top of the Palafour chair lifts. The route is any line you like across the mountainside beneath the lines of the twin three-seater Palafour lifts. The uppermost section can be very patchy, since these slopes are in full sun most of the day. If you are lucky enough to visit when conditions are good, pick your way carefully past the rocky outcrops surrounding the uppermost section to begin the best fall-line descent, before sweeping to the right across the slopes to join the Combe/Gentiane/Anémone merged home-run blues beside La Savouna mountain restaurant. By crossing these main pistes you can reach the Chardonnet button lift by the roadside below right, as well as the upper end of Le Bec Rouge; or join them to return to Tignes-le-Lac base.

LYS

Leaving the Palafour lifts, the wide, gentle, reception piste splits in two: keeping ahead left is the start of the Anémone blue piste; the Lys peels off to the right. The Lys is really just a gentle broad-link piste down to the base of the Aiguille Percée and Merles chair lifts, making only one wide turn to get there and joined from above right by the Bruyères blue. The approach to the Aiguille Percée chair lift, below right, is an easy link. The Anémone piste converges from above left here too, and it is possible to join it to continue back to Tignes-le-Lac. The Lys ends with a flat link over to the Merles chair lift in the Chardonnet lakes plateau below right.

AIGUILLE PERCÉE CHAIR LIFT

7 mins

- 304 m (997 ft) vertical rise
- 1121 m (1226 yd) long
- 1430 passengers/hour

This lift reaches the highest point in the sector and the journey up has good views to the eponymous rock formation itself, in the crown of pinnacles that surmounts this area. On arrival, turn right for all links; there are good directional signs here, plus a piste-patrol information/first-aid cabin. The views are terrific: over the Palet sector towards La Grande Motte and La Grande Casse to one side, and down the line of the Marais chair lift towards La Grande Sassière on the horizon at the Italian border on the other.

The Corniche blue begins by flowing directly off this highest point beside the arrival point of the nearby Marais chair lift, towards l'Aiguille Percée and all routes to Les Brévières and Les Boisses; U-turning to the right under the line of the arriving Aiguille Percée accesses the Cyclamen red back down the lift-line.

CYCLAMEN

As soon as you pass under the line of the arriving Aiguille Percée chair lift, the Cyclamen begins to earn its red grade with a short, sharp drop. Once started, go high off to the left for some lovely steep and deep freeride on the far side of the lift-line. Alternatively, after the good red start, the piste mellows out to a fast schuss towards a Y-junction: the short, gentle Bruyères blue variation begins wide out to the left; the Cyclamen continues ahead right. This mid-section is a fast, wide motorway with a milder red profile. The open powder fields and natural quarters under the lift-line give a more challenging variation. All routes make good links with the Aiguille Percée lift and also join the Anémone and Lys blues for the onward descent.

ANÉMONE/GENTIANE/COMBE

The Anémone begins at the top of the Palafour chair lifts, ahead left at the junction for the Lys blue, for a broad blue cruise towards the Aiguille Percée chair lift.

Approaching the lift, veer left to continue the descent. The Lys blue rejoins from the right and you could take this straight on to reach the Merles chair lift into the Palet sector, although this is a very flat link. As the Anémone curves to the left, Tignes-le-Lac and Le Bec Rouge come into view and the piste divides into two. The narrower, steeper variation into the gully to the left is the Combe; the Gentiane is effectively all the high ground in between, with plenty of opportunity for crossover variations. All routes continue straight towards Tignes-le-Lac base, passing La Savouna mountain restaurant on the way. Keep highest right to ride over to Le Bec Rouge and to reach the Chardonnet button lift.

CORNICHE

This is a good varied blue spilling off the small plateau at the top of the Aiguille Percée and Marais chair lifts. The distinctive l'Aiguille Percée rock is visible from here and is easy to reach, either for a great vantage point over the Tignes domain, or to access the Naturide route on the far side of the col.

The Corniche follows the lift-line, with a steepish start before flowing out as a wide schuss; freeriding off to the left will give you a seriously steep start into the Vallon de la Sache. Alternatively, keep on the piste to reach the entrance for the Sache black ahead left. Continuing on the Corniche, now swinging much more gently to the right, then takes you to the entrance for the Silène black. The Corniche is very flat at this point, requiring a schuss to keep up momentum to carry you over the watershed towards Tignes-le-Lac or Les Boisses. Once over this crest, the piste picks up a decent gradient, straight past the entrance for the Myosotis red and arriving Aiguille Rouge chair lift. The final section of the Corniche heads directly towards l'Alpage restaurant level for all onward options from that point.

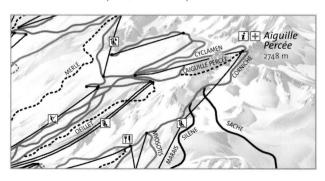

L'AIGUILLE PERCÉE & NATURIDE

The 'pierced needle': this impressive geological oddity is well worth a visit and is one of this sector's highlights. It is easy to reach from the top of the Aiguille Percée and Marais chair lifts, by riding under the Marais lift-line to access the high contour-line traverse towards it. The traverse track is usually well defined, the final approach needing just a short climb or side step up to see through the void in the rock. It is a uniquely beautiful site for contemplating the stunning surroundings, with vistas over almost the entire Tignes domain and towards the upper Val d'Isère sectors in the far distance.

There is a narrow col just a little further on too, for the easiest access to the Naturide on the other side. The Naturide descent begins from wherever you can safely climb down to the slopes beyond. The ungroomed route is a very mild black, but the tricky

access gives it the edge. It is quite short too, veering over to the right to join the Bruyères blue piste towards the base of the Aiguille Percée chair lift and all onward options. A better alternative, and to extend the ride, is to aim for the arrival point of the twin Palafour chair lifts below right, picking up the route of the Oeillet Naturide from there to deliver an almost summit-to-base freeride descent.

● *Traverse to l'Aiguille Percée*

SACHE

As soon as you see the Espace Killy piste map, you are drawn to this long, solitary black, ranging far away from the core ski area: it promises an memorable tour, but it needs work to deliver.

The start, off the upper Corniche blue piste at l'Aiguille Percée, is no more than a fair red, and the whole upper half of the run is quite tame. The most challenging start is to leave the Corniche early and drop off to the left to ride down to join the Sache below: this provides a seriously steep and deep adrenaline rush to kick the run off with a bang. Another good option is to continue on the Corniche until the Silène black, then leave to the left to freeride over the steeper open powder fields to join the Sache.

The mid-section is just a blue equivalent cruise, heading straight towards the piste-side emergency radio-phone hut. The route then gradually begins to drop down into the main valley, narrowing over more varied terrain. Off to the left of the piste is some great freeride potential, with lots of natural kickers in the steeper and deeper powder, but do not go too low because the river narrows into a severe gorge below left. The piste has been a vast motorway up to this point, but now the real fun begins. The fall-line gradient increases abruptly and the route starts to earn its true black grading, narrowing considerably and twisting and turning off the shoulder of the mountain into the wooded valley, often with huge moguls crumpling the piste, the challenge building with every turn.

The Sache ends when it drops out on to the Pavot red route below, but the descent continues as this good thigh-burning red, still turning and twisting down the wooded slopes before the final schuss out to Les Brévières base on the Pitots blue – an epic descent of 1156 m (3793 ft).

SILÈNE

On the piste map, this is another promising looking black at the margins of the ski domain. It is certainly worth investigating, but to be honest it is no more than a fair red. The entrance, off the Corniche blue, and the upper section are just a blue equivalent. A good alternative is to ride off to the left, over the undulating powder fields down to join the much more exciting Sache.

The Silène does pick up a better gradient, becoming a worthwhile run on its short lower section, often with a reasonable mogul field and with plenty of opportunity to ride off left (best) and right into the deeper powder at the sides. The route finishes by converging with the Myosotis red to make a good link with the Marais and Aiguille Rouge chair lifts. Swinging left above the lifts base joins the Mélèzes blue towards Les Boisses, and Les Brévières.

MYOSOTIS

This is a short run, but definitely the best true red in this area and worth a blast, making a particularly good first real red for early intermediates. The run begins at the top of the Aiguille Rouge chair lift, but is easily accessed using the Corniche blue, too. This mountainside is shared with the Silène black, which is wide out to the left. The Myosotis is therefore a twin of the Silène's best lower section, taking a good fall-line descent parallel to the lift-lines.

The upper section is broad, with a fair red profile. The mid-section narrows and has a couple of bends to take the sting out of the steeper gradient, before schussing out to easy links with the Marais and Aiguille Rouge chair lifts below; caution to the right as the Rhododendron blue joins and crosses your line of descent – swing left with it to head towards Les Boisses or Les Brévières.

RHODODENDRON

This begins at the top of the Chaudannes chair lift, and from the end of the Corniche piste, as a motorway blue shared with traffic heading for the Petit Col blue. After the initial broad swoop towards the junction for the Petit Col, which departs to the right, the Rhododendron swings left to continue as a good wide blue, with a couple of sweeping bends before running out above the Marais Plateau, across the line of the Myosotis and Silène pistes to become the Mélèzes blue. The piste splits down to the right under the line of the Aiguille Rouge chair lift, to link with it and the Marais chair lift below, merged with the Myosotis red – be cautious when merging and crossing.

Another option is to ride high to the right just after the junction for the Petit Col. It is not too steep, but is good on powder

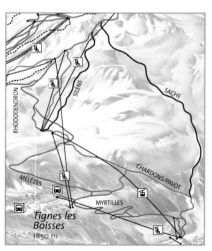

days because it takes you over some lovely open, undulating terrain towards easy links with the same two lifts below. The route is a good blue and provides a great excursion for competent novices when combined with the Mélèzes and Myrtilles blues all the way to Les Brévières.

CHARDONS/PAVOT

Accessed via the uppermost section of the Mélèzes blue, flowing off the Marais Plateau to the left of the Sache gondola's upper station. Keep high to the left if travelling from the Rhododendron, Myosotis or Silène pistes because the ground around the gondola station is very flat. The route swings to the right, under the line of the gondola, developing a steeper and narrower pitch as it heads towards the junction for the Chardons red ahead left; the Mélèzes continues to the right under the line of the Boisses chair lift.

The Chardons begins with a slightly steeper dip to the left, but then runs out to become simply a narrow flat trail through the woods. It is really just a link track and would be hard work on a board. As it passes above the hamlet of Les Boisses, there is a choice: either finish the Chardons by turning right for the final short, steep straight down to the roadside and Boisses chair lift below, or continue straight on following the flat forest trail, which is now called the Pavot red.

The Pavot is exactly the same as the earlier Chardons, often requiring a skate to keep momentum. The final section of the trail at last begins to use gravity, maintaining a straight and narrow line but allowing a build-up of speed to arrive at a tight right-hand bend where the epic Sache black run drops abruptly in to join from above left.

This now shared final descent is worth the hike to get here: twisting and turning down the steep, forested mountainside for a short but challenging workout, with frequent lumps and bumps, and eventually being joined from the right by the Myrtilles blue coming from Les Boisses (caution for traffic emerging) to schuss out towards Les Brévières base straight ahead. The Sache gondola base station is on the right below.

MÉLÈZES

This is a sheltered, tree-lined blue, flowing out of the Marais Plateau and past the upper station of the Sache gondola. The route swings under the line of the gondola to a junction where the Chardons red route leaves sharply to the left. Keep straight on veering right, under the line of the chair lift, to remain on the Mélèzes. From this narrower traverse, the route widens into a broader straight, looking directly towards the Lac du Chevril, then makes a hairpin bend to the left, narrowing considerably and developing a fair red character after heavy use. Approaching the hamlet of Les Boisses, either drop off on the steeper pitch to the right, or continue traversing under the line of the chair lift for a gentler route down, joined by the Chardons red for the final easy link to the roadside and Boisses chair lift.

The ski-bus stop for Tignes is approximately a 100 m (109 yd) walk up the road on the right, handy late in the day if you are in danger of missing the last lifts.

The Myrtilles blue continues the descent to Les Brévières, beginning to the left just above the chair lift.

MYRTILLES

This is basically just a mountain track from Les Boisses down to Les Brévières, twisting and turning down the side of the valley to keep a gentle gradient, although you can take steeper shortcuts between the bends. The mid-section, particularly as you pass under the line of the Sache gondola, is very flat and would be a hike on a board.

The track eventually emerges out of the woods to join the Pavot red for the final schuss down to the right to Les Brévières.

⬟ *The Lac du Chevril, glimpsed through the woods by the Mélèzes blue*

LES BRÉVIÈRES

This is an attractive village nestled deep in the Isère Valley, at the lowest point in the Espace Killy (1550 m/5086 ft), and dominated by the massive wall of the Tignes Barrage, which dams the Isère River. Only two lifts are needed to reach the pistes above Tignes and, as described in the preceding pages, there are three home runs to the edge of the village.

🔺 *Les Brévières village*

Approaching by piste brings you directly to the lifts' base, on the opposite side of the river from the village centre. The Sache gondola and Brévières chair lift are immediately to the right and there is an attractive piste-side restaurant (l'Etoile des Neiges) on the left. Two short drag lifts on the far side of the gondola station serve a gentle pisted zone designated as the beginners' area. These lifts are free of charge and do not require a ski pass to use them. Snow conditions at this low altitude do suffer quickly in warmer weather and deteriorate rapidly when there has been no fresh snow, but the area is covered by snow-making equipment and is well maintained to keep the home runs open.

A short bridge leads straight ahead into the heart of the village: a cluster of pleasant small bar/restaurants creates a focus to the centre, and there is a post office (with a cash machine), a small supermarket, an ESF ski-school office and tourist information office, as well as a number of small hotels and pensions. Parking is free in the open car parks at both ends of the village.

SACHE GONDOLA

9³/₄ mins ▲▼

- 622 m (2041 ft) vertical rise
- 1908 m (2087 yd) long
- 1500 passengers/hour

The base station has a ski-pass kiosk and photo booth, an electronic information board and large-scale piste map; the gondola is accessible to pedestrians. The journey up gives a good vantage point to view the painted image on the wall of the dam.

On arrival, exit the building straight ahead to emerge on the wide Marais Plateau, linking on-piste straight ahead towards the easy links with the Marais and Aiguille Rouge chair lifts.

BRÉVIÈRES CHAIR LIFT

10 mins

- 270 m (886 ft) vertical rise
- 1077 m (1178 yd) long
- 720 passengers/hour
- Free for pedestrians

This is a slow old fixed chair, connecting the villages of Les Brévières and Les Boisses, arriving near the roadside a short walk from Les Boisses 'centre'. On arrival, either dismount straight ahead to walk to the roadside, or U-turn to the right to go over the pisted footbridge over the road to connect with the Boisses chair lift below right.

BOISSES CHAIR LIFT

8¹/₄ mins

- 409 m (1342 ft) vertical rise
- 1180 m (1291 yd) long
- 900 passengers/hour
- Closed 11.00–noon

Great views over the Lac du Chevril and right up the Isère Valley towards the Col de l'Iseran on the journey up, arriving at the Marais Plateau, at the side of the Sache gondola upper station. Dismount straight ahead – all onward links as per Sache gondola.

MARAIS CHAIR LIFT

3 | **15½ mins** | • 556 m (1824 ft) vertical rise
• 2239 m (2449 yd) long
• 1100 passengers/hour

This is another slow fixed chair but, considering the length of the lift-line and huge vertical rise, it provides a very useful link to the highest lift-accessible altitude in this sector. The lift departs from the lowest edge of the Marais Plateau, just below and to the right of the Aiguille Rouge chair lift. The mid- to upper-section of the journey dips down into the Vallon de la Sache, travelling parallel to the Corniche blue run, giving a fantastic view of l'Aiguille Percée silhouetted against the skyline above left. On arrival, dismount straight ahead to start the Cyclamen red piste (to link towards the Palet sector and both Tignes bases), or U-turn right to begin the Corniche blue and to access l'Aiguille Percée and the Sache and Silène blacks. A piste-patrol information/first-aid cabin is located on this small arrival plateau.

AIGUILLE ROUGE CHAIR LIFT

4 | **7¼ mins** | • 315 m (1034 ft) vertical rise
• 1026 m (1122 yd) long
• 2000 passengers/hour

This lift departs from the Marais Plateau, just above the level of the Marais chair lift, and specifically serves the good Myosotis red piste that runs parallel down the lift-line. There is a tool point at the get-on area. The lift arrives on the side of the final section of the Corniche blue piste. Dismount to the left to join the flow of the piste towards l'Alpage/Lo Soli restaurant and all routes to Tignes-le-Lac (or back to the Marais Plateau via the Rhododendron blue), or U-turn left for the best start on the Myosotis red.

PETIT COL

This is accessed via the Rhododendron blue, from the area behind l'Alpage/Lo Soli restaurant, at the top of the Chaudannes chair lift, and at the finish of the Corniche run. After the wide shared start, veer right for the Petit Col. The piste flows over the watershed to truly begin on the steep slopes beyond, taking a twisting route to lessen the gradient, before swinging right to take a gentler path across the hillside. The finish merges into the Bleuets and Stade de Slalom pistes, crossing the line of the Almes button lift to traverse directly across to Tignes-le-Lac at the base of the Palafour and Millonex lifts. Another option, before you reach the Almes lift, is to turn left to follow the Bleuets access track, to swoop under the road through the pisted tunnel for good links with the Chaudanne and Paquis chair lifts immediately beyond.

BLEUETS

A busy home run to Tignes-le-Lac, beginning beside l'Alpage/ Lo Soli mountain restaurant, with panoramic views over Tignes. This is a wide piste, but quickly gets chopped up from heavy use and deserves its red status. The Èpilobes Naturide begins to the left, once past the restaurant terrace, but this is really just an ungroomed variation swinging wide out to the left to join the Petit Col blue; worth a go on powder days, of course. The Bleuets sweeps straight down, funnelling through a cutting in a rocky outcrop ahead, before veering to the right towards Tignes-le-Lac. The final section traverses across the base area lift-lines and Stade de Slalom pistes, as per the Petit Col, or you can take the Bleuets blue link track to the left to run under the main road, via a pisted tunnel, to link with the Chaudannes and Paquis chair lifts.

POINT-TO-POINT ROUTES: COMPETENT NOVICES

TIGNES-LE-LAC » VAL CLARET (VIA PALET SECTOR)

Palafour chair lift → Lys → Merles chair lift → Grattalu → Carline

VAL CLARET » TIGNES-LE-LAC (VIA PALET SECTOR)

Tichot chair lift → Carline → Grattalu chair lift → Lac

Grand Huit chair lift → Perce-neige → Anémone/Gentiane

TIGNES-LE-LAC » LA GRANDE MOTTE

Link track → Paquis chair lift → Piste 'H' → Prariond/Bollin → Grande Motte funicular

LA GRANDE MOTTE » TIGNES-LE-LAC

Génépy → Prariond → Cafo → Tufs chair lift → Aeroski gondola

VAL CLARET CENTRE » VAL D'ISÈRE

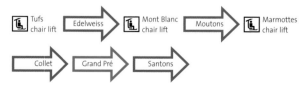

Tufs chair lift → Edelweiss → Mont Blanc chair lift → Moutons → Marmottes chair lift

Collet → Grand Pré → Santons

VAL D'ISÈRE » VAL CLARET CENTRE

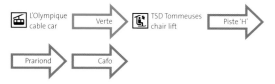

TIGNES-LE-LAC » LES BRÉVIÈRES

LES BRÉVIÈRES » TIGNES-LE-LAC

TIGNES-LE-LAC » VAL D'ISÈRE

VAL D'ISÈRE » TIGNES-LE-LAC – SEE PAGE 143

POINT-TO-POINT ROUTES: GOOD INTERMEDIATES AND ABOVE

TIGNES-LE-LAC » LA GRANDE MOTTE

Aeroski gondola → Piste 'H' → Campanules → Piste 'H' → Prariond/Bollin

Grande Motte funicular

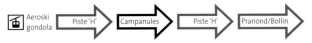

LA GRANDE MOTTE » TIGNES-LE-LAC (VIA PALET SECTOR)

Face → Double 'M' → Tichot chair lift → Carline → Grattalu chair lift

Lac → Grand Huit chair lift → Ancolie → Anémone/Combe

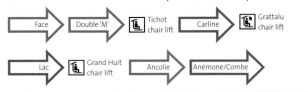

TOVIÈRE » LA DAILLE (VAL D'ISÈRE SECTOR)

Rocs → Creux → Verte → Semanmille button lift → Piste 'G'

Raye

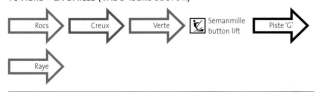

LA DAILLE (VAL D'ISÈRE SECTOR) » TOVIÈRE

Funival funicular → OK → Verte → TSD Tommeuses chair lift

VAL CLARET CENTRE » VAL D'ISÈRE

Tufs chair lift → Edelweiss → OK → Diebold → Funival funicular → Face

VAL D'ISÈRE » VAL CLARET CENTRE

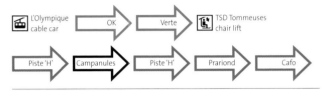

L'Olympique cable car → OK → Verte → TSD Tommeuses chair lift

Piste 'H' → Campanules → Piste 'H' → Prariond → Cafo

TIGNES-LE-LAC » LES BRÉVIÈRES

Palafour chair lift → Lys → Aiguille Percée chair lift → Corniche → Sache

Pavot → Pitots

LES BRÉVIÈRES » TIGNES-LE-LAC

Sache gondola → Link track → Aiguille Rouge chair lift → Corniche → Bleuets

Stade de slalom

TIGNES-LE-LAC » VAL D'ISÈRE

VAL D'ISÈRE » TIGNES-LE-LAC – SEE PAGE 144

MOUNTAIN BARS & RESTAURANTS

For such an expansive ski area, Tignes doesn't actually have a lot of on-piste restaurants, but they're well spaced out and you are never more than a couple of runs or a lift away from a refuelling and refreshment point. All offer food service from around 11.30–15.00 hours, but provide a full bar service and snacks all day; all have WCs, most of these are serviced and levy a small charge.

LA GRANDE MOTTE SECTOR

There are two on-mountain restaurant sites serving Tignes' signature mountain area. Both are accessible by pedestrians too.

Le Panoramique €€ A huge establishment occupying virtually the entire arrival area at the funicular upper station at 3032 m (9948 ft). There is a fair-sized terrace furnished with bench-style tables/seating; unfortunately, because the terrace is immediately outside the funicular station, a train-load of passengers disgorges every few minutes and traipses across it, but at least it's buzzing.

Inside, there is a bar, a large self-service restaurant and a separate à la carte restaurant; the interior of the bar and self-service dining area are pleasant but rather dimly lit, with little natural daylight. The self-service food selection is wide, with a good salad buffet, a reasonable choice of ready-made starters, lighter bites and around a dozen hot dishes, including daily specials; a good selection of fresh desserts and fresh fruit; canned and bottled drinks and a fair wine list. Microwaves are available for reheating food that is cooling too quickly on the coldest days.

◐ Enjoying the warm sun and a cool beer on l'Alpage terrace, L'Aiguille Percée

Gourmand €€+ This is the fine dining restaurant at Le Panoramique, at the 3032 m (9948 ft) services area. The venue is situated in a much cosier separate section at the rear of the self-service building, but with a fair amount of natural daylight in the interior; maitre d' service on entering from Le Panoramique. The attractive, quality decor evokes a rustic chalet feel, with an open fire grill (chef attended) and a cheese/dessert display on an antique farm cart in the centre of the dining room. The menu is of high quality, with a wide selection of starters and main courses, including Savoyard specialities and a choice of refined meat and fish dishes, complemented by a very good wine list; table service throughout. Reservations are necessary, except at the quietest low season dates. ☎ +33 (0)4 79 06 47 21

Le Chalet du Bollin €€ Situated piste-side on the Prariond/Bollin blue home run just above Val Claret base, slightly below the level of, but on the opposite side of the piste from, the Bollin chairlift arrival point. Enter via the fair-sized piste-side terrace, which is served by a snacks/drinks counter and furnished with bench-style tables/seating and a fair number of deckchairs. The chalet-style interior is reasonably attractive, with a full bar and two segregated dining areas: one with a standard menu offering basic fare such as salads, steak and chips, pastas and filled baguettes; the other to the rear of the building offering an à la carte service, featuring Savoyard specialities and slightly more refined versions of the main restaurant dishes. ☎ +33 (0)4 79 06 46 44

There are also a number of piste-accessible venues at Val Claret, both at the main base area near the funicular station and at Val Claret Centre at the base of the Tufs and Claret lifts.

TOVIÈRE SECTOR

Just the one venue in this sector, but it is hard to miss because it's situated right on the summit of La Tovière. Pedestrians can also get here using the gondola.

La Tovière €+ A plain but attractive older building, with an authentic mountain refuge feel and commanding views from the terrace over the entire upper La Daille and Bellevarde sectors of Val d'Isère. There are a couple of serving hatches providing a drinks/snacks service on the side terrace nearest the gondola platform; the main terrace is at the front of the building. The interior is divided into two: a reasonably attractive self-service restaurant offering an unpretentious selection of wholesome, carb-loaded fare, including soup, spaghetti bolognese, steak and chips, ham and eggs, and so on; the other side of the building is a fairly spacious but cosy saloon bar with an open fire. The nicest place to sit inside is the mezzanine area. ☎ +33 (0)4 79 06 35 05

PALET SECTOR

Again, just the one venue in this sector, but it's right in the middle of the ski area at the base of the Grattalu and Col du Palet lifts.

Le Palet €+ This has a huge metal-grid terrace with views towards the imposing La Grande Casse and Aiguille Noire de Pramecou. The restaurant building is modern in design with traditional materials/influences. There is a snacks/drinks kiosk on the terrace; a bright, attractive interior bar; and a self-service restaurant. The main restaurant food selection is based around a core of basic snack-orientated fare, including sausage and chips, hamburgers, quiche, lasagne and spaghetti bolognese. ☎ +33 (0)4 79 06 46 06

L'AIGUILLE PERCÉE SECTOR

Two restaurants here, both easily accessible and overlooking the Tignes-le-Lac side of the mountains.

L'Alpage des Chaudannes/Lo Soli €€ These are situated next to the Chaudannes chair lift arrival point and accessible by pedestrians, in an attractive stone chalet with a big wood-decked sun-terrace and bench tables/seating and deckchairs; there are far-reaching vistas over the Tignes domain, . The fair-sized interior is decorated in a homely chalet style. There is a choice of two restaurants: **l'Alpage** is the larger self-service option, offering a good range of standard meat and vegetable dishes, pasta and salads; **Lo Soli** is the separate à la carte restaurant, housed in a lovely separate dining room with an open fire and low wood-beamed ceilings for cosy lunches on cold days, plus a terrace for sunny days. The menu isn't extensive, but it is well balanced and features traditional mountain fare. ❶ +33 (0)4 79 06 07 42

La Savouna €€ This is one of Tignes' original mountain restaurants, situated piste-side on the Combe/Gentiane/Anémone home runs just above Le Bec Rouge, with a small terrace overlooking the passing pistes, resorts and lake; some deckchairs. The compact interior is rather plain and old-fashioned, but has the feel of a welcoming mountain refuge; full bar and snack-orientated food. The restaurant also opens some evenings, with Ratrack transport from Tignes-le-Lac. Descent afterwards is by sliding down the piste inside a plastic bin liner – honest! Great fun after a few vins chauds. ❶ +33 (0)4 79 06 33 80

▶ *Afternoon sunbathing at Val Claret Centre*

ALTERNATIVE ACTIVITIES

Tignes also provides a good range of other activities to complement the principal piste-based sports; mostly focused on extreme
sports, but with plenty of tamer activities to appeal to all ages
and abilities too. Full details and bookings are available via the
Maison de Tignes tourist offices in each resort; Evolution2
adventure centres ⓦ www.evolution2.com ① +33 (0)4 79 06 35 76;
and/or the Bureau des Guides de Tignes ① +33 (0)4 79 06 42 76
ⓘ Activities may not be covered by travel insurance (see page 50).

LANGLAUF

Tignes' prime focus is on Alpine skiing, but cross-country skiing
(ski du fond) is not completely overlooked. Circuits are located in
three very different settings: a simple short blue circuit around
the frozen lake between the two Tignes resorts; a more testing
high-altitude red circuit on the glacier on La Grande Motte; and
a red-graded forest trail at Les Brévières. Nordic enthusiasts are
also well catered for at Val d'Isère (see page 159).

SNOWSHOEING

Referred to locally as raquettes, snowshoes are the best way for
all visitors to get out into the wilder, more tranquil corners of the
mountains where you are more likely to spot the Alpine wildlife,
such as ibex, chamois, dahu and marmottes, which shy away from
the busier and noisier resort margins.

Modern snowshoes are made of lightweight materials and are
very easy to master: they work by spreading your weight over a
wider surface area, allowing you to walk more easily over deep
snow, using a pair of ski poles for balance. Equipment hire is
available at most good ski rental shops.

SKI JÖRING

The frozen lakes of many Alpine and Scandinavian winter resorts feature this exciting snowsport, yet you may never have encountered it before. Imagine waterskiing, but swap the boat for a horse, trotting around a specially prepared circuit on Tignes' frozen lake and pulling skiers behind on specially-adapted long reins. An exhilarating action sport, especially when your confidence grows and you let the animals get into a full gallop; best for experienced skiers, although tamer trots for novices can be arranged. Duration: 30 minutes. Details at the tourist office.

ICE DIVING

A stunning activity and a unique opportunity to glimpse the hidden world beneath the frozen surface of Tignes lake. Wearing a special 'dry suit' and scuba gear, you are guided through a hole in the ice to plunge into the unworldly eerie blueness below. Full pre-dive training is given and the activity is open to all; you are accompanied at all times by an instructor and follow a safety tether whilst under the ice. A must-do activity for adventure sports enthusiasts and a real conversation stopper. Actual dive after training session lasts around 20 minutes. For further information, check out ⓦ www.plongee-tignes.fr.st

🔺 *Ice diving at Tignes lake*

ICE SKATING

There is a full-size, outdoor, natural ice rink at Tignes-le-Lac, just by the side of the lake near the Aeroski gondola. The facility is open every day from 14.00–19.00 hours; skate hire is available on-site.

SNOWMOBILES

This thrilling motorsport is consistently the most requested alternative wintersports activity. There is a dedicated circuit marked out on the open mountainside between the Almes and Marais areas just above Tignes-le-Lac; accessible on-piste during the day using the Petit Col blue run or in the evenings by Ratrack. Each Ski-Doo can carry two people, drive the machine yourself or hang on tight as a passenger. Charged per machine.

DOG SLEIGHS

A wonderful activity accessible to all: teams of husky and Samoyed dogs pull passengers in Arctic sleds guided by an experienced musher around the frozen lake in central Tignes. Mushing lessons are available to teach you how to control the dogs and steer the sled on your own, or you can just sit back and enjoy the ride. Half-day excursions through the peaceful wooded trails around the nearby village of Sainte-Foy-en-Tarentaise are also available.

○ *Mushing on the frozen lake at Tignes*

AQUA CENTRE

This centre is a welcome recent addition to the range of sports and leisure facilities in Tignes. Located on the shore of the lake, nearest Le Bec Rouge, it is easily reached on foot from the rest of Tignes-le-Lac. Features: 25 m (82 ft) swimming pool, water slides, jacuzzis, Turkish baths, saunas, gymnasium and fitness suite.

FLYING

Tignes offers various ways to take to the air and share an eagle's-eye view of the Alps.

Helicopter drop-offs on mountain summits are banned in France, so Tignes has come up with a unique way of bending the rules to permit a reverse version of heliskiing: accompanied by specialist off-piste instructors and equipped with avalanche transceivers, you take the ski lift to the summit of La Tovière before descending via the north-facing gullies all the way down into the tree line at the Bois de la Laye on the shores of the Lac du Chevril, where you are then picked up by helicopter for the return to resort. Full-on heli-skiing trips into nearby Italy are permissible. Tamer, but no less breathtaking, sightseeing trips are also available.

Airplane sightseeing flights are available over the Espace Killy, the surrounding Olympic resorts and even over the summit of Mont Blanc, Western Europe's highest peak. The Aeroclub du Palet have a hangar and specially pisted runway next to the Col des Ves chair lift in the Palet sector. ☎ 33 (0)4 79 06 57 60

Hang-gliding and/or paragliding are other flying options. Launch off from the glacier of La Grande Motte, in tandem with a professional pilot, to soar silently above the slopes with skiers far below your feet, before landing on Tignes lake ice for a real 007 sensation. Further information ⓦ www.parapente-tignes.com

ICE CAVE

This fascinating structure was burrowed over 100 m (328 ft) into the glacier by a team of artists who have created a chamber of ephemeral artworks from the ancient ice. Backlit sculptures glow eerily in the muted light and you can leave your hand prints on a specially set-aside section of the cave wall. Situated near the 3032 m services area at the top of the funicular and accessible by pedestrians; ◕ Open daily 10.00–16.00 hours

SPECIAL EVENTS

Tignes has a good and varied programme of events, which is organized by a dedicated resort animation team; programme leaflets are printed on a weekly basis, distributed throughout the resort and available from the tourist offices. Since this high-altitude setting is subject to frequent severe weather, the resort also has a contingency plan in place for days when rough weather forces the closure of the ski lifts: an additional programme of free daytime entertainment swings into action and details are communicated to all hotels and apartment receptions, posted in the tourist offices and broadcast on the local radio (Radio Tignes Europe2: 88.2fm in Les Brévières and Les Boisses; 92.2fm in Tignes).

NIGHT SKIING

Over Christmas, New Year and the February school holidays, floodlight skiing is available on the town base slopes at Val Claret Centre, Tignes-le-Lac and Les Brévières. Pistes and lifts remain open until 19.30 hours and access is free to all current Tignes/Espace Killy ski-pass holders.

APRÈS-SKI

🔺 *Festival fireworks over Val Claret*

When the sun sets, the emphasis shifts from the pistes to the facilities and ambiance of the resorts, but Tignes continues its addiction to activity: it's possible to ski on some evenings during the week and the resorts also have a number of spa facilities to pummel and pamper visitors. Tignes' commitment to mountain sports is its major attraction and, unlike its more fashionable and trendy neighbour, it doesn't have a reputation for raucous night-life; but there's certainly plenty of choice available, particularly in Val Claret Centre, and on the right night with the right crowd the après-ski scene can be as lively as anywhere else in the Alps.

BOWLING & GAMES ARCADE

A full-size ten-pin bowling complex (10 lanes) is located beside the Tignespace sports centre, on the lakeside road level at Le Bec Rouge at the far side of the main road tunnel. The building also houses a bar, nightclub, pool tables and arcade video-games' machines, and is a real focus of activity in the evenings for young locals and visitors alike. Bowling lanes should be booked in advance: ☎ +33 (0)4 79 06 39 95

SOIRÉE PANORAMIQUE

One evening per week (normally Thursday) the Panoramique restaurant, in the glacial zone at 3032 m (9948 ft) on La Grande Motte, hosts a high-altitude dinner featuring typical Savoyard specialities such as raclette and fondue. Homemade patisseries, wine and coffee are included in the set price, which includes transport via the funicular; for a small supplement you can opt to make the unmissable night-time ski descent to Val Claret holding a flaming torch to light your way. The funicular departs from the Val Claret base station at 20.00 hours; bookings must be made before 18.00 hours; torchlight descent option is only available to good parallel skiers and competent snowboarders and is accompanied by qualified guides; subject to favourable weather conditions. For reservations ☎ +33 (0)4 79 06 47 21

PAMPERING

The trend for 'wellness' holidays in the Alpine resorts continues to grow and the available facilities are improving all the time. Many of the larger 3- and 4-star quality hotels have their own in-house hydrotherapy suites, usually attached to fitness rooms; additionally, Tignes also has two major spas, one in each resort.
🕐 Open daily 10.00–20.00 hours.
Les Bains du Montana: this spa in Les Almes at Tignes-le-Lac (based at the hotel Village Montana) has an outdoor heated swimming pool, Jacuzzi, sauna and Turkish bath; bath towels are provided. The spa also has a beauty suite offering sports and relaxing massages, lymphatic drainage, facials, body moisturizing and toning wrap treatments, manicures, pedicures and waxing. Spa facilities are available all day; treatments must be pre-booked.
☎ +33 (0)4 79 40 05 12

Aquatonic in Val Claret: based at the aparthotel Résidence l'Ecrin des Neiges, this offers cardio-fitness and weight-training gymnasium; an 'aquagym' pool for resistance exercise against a counter-current; water jets and hydrotherapy treatments; Jacuzzi, sauna and Turkish bath and a range of beauty treatments, including facials, body moisturizing and toning, manicures, reflexology, pedicures and waxing. Spa facilities are available all day; treatments must be pre-booked. ❶ +33 (0)4 79 40 25 56

RETAIL THERAPY

Tignes is an extensive conurbation with a year-round population and therefore has a fair range of shops, although, like all ski resorts, most of these are mountain sports equipment and clothing stores. The main shopping areas are the Gallerie du Palafour at Le Bec Rouge in Tignes-le-Lac and around the rue de Front de Neige and place du Curling in Val Claret Centre, with further small retail clusters on the promenade de Tovière in Tignes-le-Lac le Rosset and on the lower road level near the ski bus terminal at Val Claret (see town plans on pages 181 and 183). As well as the usual plethora of sports outlets, both resort centres also have a fair number of boutiques, regional products delicatessens, patisseries and bakeries, souvenir shops and several well-stocked large supermarkets; also a couple of pharmacies/perfumeries, specialist eyewear boutiques, newsagents, bookshops and photographic studios. There are several banks, most with 24-hour cash machines, a post office in each resort centre (also with ATMs) and a number of launderettes.

Thursdays and Sundays are market days: from early morning until early evening the promenade de Tovière in Tignes-le-Lac le Rosset is lined with traders' stalls, some selling regional products.

CAFÉS & RESTAURANTS

Tignes has plenty of snack bars and cafés and more than 60 restaurants. A lot of the restaurants offer similar international fare heavily reliant on pizzas and snack-orientated menus, however there are a good number of more committed and noteworthy serious restaurants too. Most are open at lunchtime and in the evenings from 19.00–24.00 hours. The following are a selection of some of the best (see town plans on pages 181 and 183).

TIGNES-LE-LAC

L'Arbina €€+ An attractive hotel on the promenade de Tovière at le Rosset, housing two well-regarded venues: a large, popular brasserie on the ground floor and a quality à la carte restaurant on the first floor. The brasserie has rapid and attentive service, wood-fire oven pizzas, salads, pastas and mixed grills, plus Savoyard specialities. The excellent à la carte restaurant offers a more gastronomic menu featuring refined interpretations of regional dishes, supported by a very extensive wine list. Both floors have terraces overlooking the lake and towards La Grande Motte; good-value lunchtime set menus. ☎ +33 (0)4 79 06 39 62 / +33 (0)4 79 06 46 83

La Ferme des 3 Capucines €€+ A restaurant housed in one of the highest altitude working dairy farms in the Alps, just off the main road at the entrance to Tignes, nearest Le Lavachet and the Paquis and Chaudannes chair lifts. The dining room is rustically decorated, with an open fire and windows looking into the cattle barns. The farm produces and serves its own cheeses and yogurts, and features home-made pastas and pastries. ☎ +33 (0)4 79 06 35 10

Le Clin d'Oeil €€ A small, intimate restaurant on the promenade de Tovière at le Rosset. Good value Savoyard and classic French dishes; good selection of wines. ☏ +33 (0)4 79 06 59 10

La Montagne (Crêpes à Gogo) € Basic café/restaurant on the promenade de Tovière at le Rosset. Handy for lunchtime snacks or afternoon coffees; recommended for its huge selection of crêpes and bruschettas. ☏ +33 (0)4 79 06 31 30

La Côte de Boeuf (Chez Bernard) €€ A simple but welcoming restaurant featuring prime fillet steaks flambéed with whisky, plus Savoyard specialities, including pierrades and braserade mixed grills. Large range of whiskys. Located in the Gallerie du Palafour at le Bec Rouge. ☏ +33 (0)4 79 06 35 81

La Chaumiere €€+ Public restaurant at the hotel Village Montana in Les Almes, accessible from the base of the Petit Col, Bleuets and Stade de Slalom pistes; quality decor and pleasant terrace. Popular lunchtime and evening venue with a good brasserie menu. ☏ +33 (0)4 79 40 01 44 ⊚ www.vmontana.com

Bagus Café €€ Pleasant small restaurant in the Gallerie du Palafour at le Bec Rouge, featuring Moroccan tajine dishes, as well as T-bone steaks and home-made pastas. ☏ +33 (0)4 79 06 49 75

Le Bouchon Montagnard €€ A cosy, quaint restaurant in the suburb of Le Lavachet. Simple, good-quality wholesome French classics and seafood dishes. Après-ski tapas with local and vintage wines, and instruments provided for any diners who are musicians. ☏ +33 (0)4 79 06 51 44

VAL CLARET

Auberge des 3 Oursons €+ Popular lunchtime venue in the Front de Neige area at Val Claret Centre. Piste-side deckchairs and terrace; interior decorated with hundreds of teddy bears. Snack-based menu, but with oysters and regional mountain fare available too; wider choice in the evenings. ☎ +33 (0)4 79 06 35 66

Le Grattalu €€ An unpretentious small restaurant focusing on good quality Savoyard specialities, including a divine fondue au chocolat with fresh fruits to dip in the bubbling chocolate. Front de Neige area of Val Claret Centre. ☎ +33 (0)4 79 06 30 78

Le Caveau €€ Attractive, cosy basement restaurant in the Front de Neige area of Val Claret Centre. It has a good range of fish and meat dishes, plus Savoyard classics; good ambiance and late night live blues music. ☎ +33 (0)4 79 06 52 32

Daffy's Cafe €€ Popular Tex Mex venue in the place du Curling in Val Claret Centre. Late night service and animated atmosphere, with a DJ at the weekend. ☎ +33 (0)4 79 06 38 75

L'Indochine €€ Vietnamese restaurant with Chinese and Thai dishes too; take-away available. In the place du Curling in Val Claret Centre. ☎ +33 (0)4 79 06 08 07

La Pignatta €€ Good quality Italian restaurant that features fresh, home-made pastas and slow-cooked Savoyard fare. Entrance from the place du Curling, in Val Claret Centre, and also from the Front de Neige. ☎ +33 (0)4 79 06 32 97

BARS & CLUBS

Both Tignes-le-Lac and Val Claret have plenty of venues (over 50 bars in total); Val Claret Centre definitely has the greatest concentration of bars and the most lively atmosphere. Most bars are open until around 01.30 hours, nightclubs until 04.00. The following are some of the most popular.

TIGNES-LE-LAC

The Red Lion British tour operator-run pub at their chalethotel Les Airelles in Les Almes. Fair programme of themes and events; SKY TV; pool table; darts; draught beers and a wide range of shots.

La Grotte du Yeti Dutch/Danish tour operator-run bar at their chalethotel near the post office opposite Le Bec Rouge. Directly accessible from the Gliss Park area pistes, at the finish of the Combe/Gentiane/Anénome runs; lively late afternoon après ski and frequent wild nights, with a good, varied programme of events, 'any excuse for a party' being the motto.

Censored Bar Lively pub with good varied theme-nights programme and frequent live music on offer. Friendly bar staff, usually outrageously attired and always working hard to make sure the evenings really rock. It is situated out in Le Lavachet, facing the ski-pass office.

Jack's Club Nightclub at the bowling centre on the lakeside level at le Bec Rouge. This whole complex is usually quite animated most nights, with Jack's open until 04.00; music policy is basically anything that seems to work for the crowd on the night.

VAL CLARET

Grizzly's Bar A really cute, almost kitsch, good bar in the Front de Neige area. Constructed and decorated with rough-hewn timber, with a large open fireplace and cosy interior, it normally has quite a chilled atmosphere, but is a real focal point in the area and therefore very trendy, so it can get lively from early afternoon right through to closing time on busy weeks.

Fish Tank Situated right in the centre of the Front de Neige area, beside the ESF office and directly accessible from the Cafo piste, so very lively around lifts' closing time. It operates as a piste-side terrace snack bar during the daytime and has a big screen for major sporting events. British draught beers and cocktails available.

Drop Zone Café Another Front de Neige venue, with a terrace easily accessible from the pistes, although the bar is tucked away inside the Sefcotel commercial gallery near the post office; with pool table, regular live music and extreme sports videos.

Le Melting Pot A nightclub with big screen music videos, DJs and regular live music – mostly Euro and House with a fair smattering of Rock. Located in the main place du Curling shopping area of Val Claret Centre. ● Open 22.00–04.00 hours
Ⓦ www.tignesmeltingpot.com

Le Blue Girl This nightclub is one of Val Claret's biggest and most raucous venues, with two bars and a 500-person capacity. Regular theme nights; infamous for its topless nights. Up-to-the-minute music policy. ● Open 23.00–04.00 hours

OUT & ABOUT
Discover Tarentaise

TARENTAISE

Although this book is a specialist guide to the Espace Killy, and given that most readers will be visiting either Val d'Isère or Tignes specifically for an one-week holiday, it would be a shame not to make a point of getting out of your resort for at least an afternoon to see more of this beautiful and important region. Being right at the end of the Tarentaise valley means there are no major non-ski-related tourist sites near to hand in winter, but this is definitely the centre of the snowsports universe and presents an almost unique opportunity to combine your trip with a day out to another world-class ski area.

The Tarentaise valley is home to three of the world's largest ski areas (Espace Killy; Paradiski; Les Trois Vallées); together these contain seven of Europe's most popular ski resorts (Val d'Isère; Tignes; Les Arcs; La Plagne; Courchevel; Méribel; Val Thorens) and these are surrounded by a multitude of further satellite stations and smaller resorts (Ste-Foy-Tarentaise; Villaroger; La Rosière, which is also linked to La Thuile in Italy; Peisey-Nancroix; Brides-les-Bains; La Tania; Champagny-en-Vanoise; Pralognan-la-Vanoise; St-Martin-de-Belleville; Les Menuires; Valmorel): offering a combined total of 1500 km (930 miles) of pistes, 500 km (310 miles) of Nordic trails and 600 ski lifts – more than enough to ensure that you won't cross your own tracks again for weeks on end.

Espace Killy ski passes of between 6 and 21 days' duration permit a free-of-charge day-pass for Paradiski, Les Trois Vallées or Valmorel; plus, reduced price day-passes at La Rosière and Ste-Foy.

ⓦ www.les3vallees.com   ⓦ www.paradiski.com
ⓦ www.valmorel.com   ⓦ www.larosiere.net
ⓦ www.saintefoy.net

ESPACE OLYMPIQUE SAVOIE

If you have your own vehicle, then it is worth considering the Espace Olympique Savoie ski pass: this is available for durations of six days or more and covers the Espace Killy; Les Trois Vallées and Paradiski, as well as a day-pass at Pralognan-la-Vanoise and Les Saisies. The passes are available from any of these stations.

LOCAL TRANSPORT

None of the other resorts are too far away. Buses and taxis are readily available and many tour operators and ski schools organize excursions to the other Tarentaise super-stations at least once a week. If you don't have your own vehicle, the easiest alternative is local bus: there are several buses per day from Val d'Isère, Tignes, Les Boisses and Les Brévières to Bourg-St-Maurice (see pages 57 and 179 for contact details); timetables are available from the resorts' tourist information offices and from the central bus/coach stations, which are located on the main road just below Val d'Isère town centre (see town plan on page 59) and on the ground floor of the Maison de Tignes-le-Lac (see town plan on page 181). Bourg-St-Maurice is the terminal train station for the Tarentaise, connected with all major valley villages, Albertville and Chambéry, as well as to the European rail network. The town is directly connected with Les Arcs by a fast funicular railway, which departs from right next to the train terminus (located near the town centre, at the side of the main through-road). Shuttles to all of the Tarentaise ski stations also depart regularly from the transport interchange at the train terminus, fares and timetables vary but the shuttle service to La Rosière's nearest chair lift is free; more information is available from the tourist office at the train station – place de la Gare, Bourg-St-Maurice. ☎ +33 (0)4 79 07 04 92

SUMMER

It may never have occurred to you before to visit a ski resort in summer. After all, what is there to do after the snow has melted? Quite a lot actually; the mountains are just as beautiful and even more accessible in summer and the glaciers are still open for skiing throughout the high summer months. Away from the glaciers, many other ski lifts also reopen during July and August to transport hikers, mountaineers and mountain bikers to the high ridges and peaks. The majority of the pistes may be green in colour now that the snow has gone, but the routes of the blue, red and black pistes still carry those gradings for downhill mountain biking; pointing your wheels rather than your ski tips or board down the fall-line takes just as much skill and guts. Horse riding, white-water sports, quad-biking and rock-climbing are just some of the other ways in which summer visitors get their kicks. The après jour in the resort bars and restaurants may be more mellow, but there are still rocking venues if you know where to look.

The explosion in high-adrenaline adventure sports has also contributed to a dramatic shift towards more 'outward-bound' pursuits and holidays. Challenging gravity is a major prerequisite for the latest thrill-seeking activities and the Alps provide the perfect setting in which to pursue them.

To escape from the stressful pace of modern life demands a more sophisticated alternative to the standard 'fly & flop' beach holiday, so why not try the natural active high of the mountains in summer? Details of all summer activities and special events are advertised on the resorts' summer websites, linked via **www.ski-ride.com** in the summer months.

◀ *The summer face of Val d'Isère*

VAL D'ISÈRE IN SUMMER

Every year in late May, the Col d'Iseran is ceremoniously opened by a convoy of snowploughs followed by motorists, motorcyclists and cyclists keen to be the first across. The pass is a stage on the Tour de France and is the highest pass on the Route des Grandes Alpes, a magnificent 684 km (425 miles) route linking Thonon-les-Bains on the shores of Lac Léman (Lake Geneva) to Menton on the Mediterranean coast. Ⓦ www.routedesgrandesalpes.com

Val d'Isère is a major tourist stop on the route and is buzzing with activity in the high summer months. Additionally, it offers a wealth of sports and cultural activities and is a summer holiday destination in its own right. Every August, the town hosts a major 4x4 motor show and has a unique high-altitude off-road driving zone on the Rocher du Bellevarde.

At La Daille, the two vertiginous rock faces of les Plates de la Daille and Roc de la Tovière are tamed by two incredible Via Ferrata routes, which consist of permanently fixed metal hand-holds/footholds and metal ropes, enabling even those who have never rock climbed before to conquer these extreme cliffs.

VANOISE NATIONAL PARK

Both Val d'Isère and Tignes are gateways to France's first national park, created in 1963 and now covering over 55,000 hectares (135,900 acres); adjoining Italy's Gran Paradiso National Park to form Western Europe's largest protected area. The park is home to endangered species such as the Alpine Ibex, chamois and bearded vulture, with over 1200 species of protected Alpine flora recorded to date within its boundaries. The highest peak in the park is La Grande Casse, at 3852m (12,638 ft), whose vertigo-inducing sheer wall dominates Tignes. Ⓦ www.vanoise.com

TIGNES IN SUMMER

Who says you need to be by the sea to sun worship on the beach? Tignes lake has its very own Plage des Sports, which is the active heart of the resort in summer and is billed as Europe's highest altitude beach, offering Hobie Cat sailing, pedaloes, canoes, fly-fishing, plus one of the most radical sports ideas around – Hot Jumping. A series of huge ramps have been built on the lakeshore near Tignes-le-Lac le Rosset, some surfaced in smooth rubber and others carpeted with dry ski matting; kitted out with a wetsuit, helmet and buoyancy aid, you propel yourself down the ramps on skis, snowboard, skateboard or roller blades, launching off high into the air to pull the slickest aerial acrobatics you can muster before splashing down into the lake. Of course, you could just spectate; the ramps area draws a big crowd and it's just as much fun to watch.

Tignes is also home to Europe's highest altitude 18-hole golf course, snaking around the slopes and encircling the lake to provide a spectacularly sited 4830 m (5282 yds) challenge for mountain loving golfers. The clubhouse sits overlooking the lake on the outskirts of Val Claret.

CAPITAL OF SUMMER SKIING

From mid June to early September, no fewer than 12 ski lifts are opened on La Grande Motte for glacier skiing, accessed directly via the funicular from Val Claret. The area boasts one of Europe's largest summer snow parks, hosting between 300–500 riders per day and positively buzzing every morning, with a chillout zone, DJs and a BBQ area to make the most of the sunbathing time too. Thousand-year-old snow and ice beneath your feet and blazing sun on your face – welcome to Europe's capital of summer skiing.

GLOSSARY

Alpine skiing: the proper name for the sport of Downhill skiing, where participants use gravity to descend the slopes; as opposed to propelling themselves along.

Arête: a sharp ridge separating two glacial valleys or cirques.

Base station: the main access point and ski lifts departure point for a particular ski area; ideally the resort itself.

Base lodge: the main services building at the base station.

Bucket lift: a type of gondola lift where passengers stand in a basic open cabin, usually installed in hilly resort centres and lower slopes areas as public transport from one sector to another.

Button lift: a type of ski lift which consists of a pole hanging from the haul cable, fitted with a circular 'button' that is placed between your legs to pull you uphill.

Carver: a type of ski that is much wider at the tips (front) and tails (rear), allowing for wide, exaggerated turns on the piste.

Cirque: a semi-circular sweep of steep mountains surrounding a generally flat high-altitude valley; a product of glacial erosion.

Couloir: a steep and usually narrow gully sometimes called a chute.

Declutchable chair lift: the fastest type of chair lift, which disconnects from the fast haul cable at the passenger get-on and get-off points to allow for easier mount/dismount.

Drag lift: generic name for all ski lifts that pull passengers along whilst they are standing on the snow.

FIS: Fédération Internationale de Ski (International Ski Federation). The governing body of snowsports, which sets rules and regulations for piste safety and international competitions.

Freeride: a form of skiing away from the pistes where participants ride wherever and however the terrain (usually extreme) allows.

Funicular: a type of railway, usually steeply inclined.

Gondola lift: a type of ski lift where passengers ride inside a small cabin. Also called a Télécabine or Telecabina in Europe; smaller versions are also known as 'bubble lifts'.

Halfpipe: a specially prepared, semi-circular, pisted trough allowing users to ride up its high side walls to perform tricks.

Kickers: ramps of snow which provide a launch point for jumping high into the air.

Langlauf: the correct term for cross-country/Nordic-style skiing where skiers propel themselves in a walking or skating motion; Langlauf skis are much longer and narrower than Alpine skis.

Magic carpet: a conveyor belt.

Mogul (mogul field): bump (series of bumps) formed after heavy use of a ski slope has left the slope deeply rutted; advanced riders relish the challenge of riding through/over these bumps.

Monoskiing: a single large ski where binding attachments are side-by-side and close together.

Nordic skiing: see Langlauf

Nursery slope: a gentle slope designated as a beginners' area.

Off-piste: skiing/snowboarding away from the prepared ski slopes.

Piste: a way-marked slope/trail, where the snow has been groomed to make it easier to ski on. Pistes are graded by difficulty and colour coded to reflect this: green runs are the easiest; blue runs are slightly more challenging but still relatively easy; red runs are difficult slopes requiring technical ability from users; black pistes are the most difficult slopes reserved for expert users.

Piste basher: a tracked snowplough vehicle, fitted with a large rake with which to groom the pistes.

Rope tow: a basic ski lift consisting of a simple loop of rope, where users just grab on to be pulled along.

Schuss: the onomatopoeic term for skiing fast down a straight slope.

Ski-Doo: trade name for a snowmobile, a tracked vehicle fitted with steerable skis resembling a motorbike.

Ski school: the generic term for an organization which provides snowsports tuition.

Slalom: a form of skiing/snowboarding involving weaving in and out of a series of spaced poles/gates, normally against the clock.

Snow Park: a specially designated area set out with ramps (kickers), halfpipes and high rails for sliding along for performing tricks.

Snowshoe: a specialized form of footwear which spreads the wearer's weight over a greater surface area, making it easier to walk over snow.

Telemark skiing: a old form of classic Alpine skiing where the skier's foot is secured to the ski binding only at the toe end, requiring the skier to flex their ankle and knee to effect turns.

Tool point: a collection of spanners and screwdrivers at a designated location on the mountain, provided to allow experienced skiers/snowboarders to adjust their own equipment.

EMERGENCIES

Emergency contact telephone numbers:

Piste security/assistance:	Val d'Isère +33 (0)4 79 06 02 10
	Tignes +33 (0)4 79 06 32 00
Medical emergencies	15
Fire	18
Police (Gendarmerie)	+33 (0)4 79 06 03 41
Hospital (Bourg St. Maurice)	+33 (0)4 79 41 79 79

In the event of a serious accident:

1. Secure the area – plant skis in the form of an 'X' slightly above the position of any casualties, or have someone stand there to warn slope traffic; protect the victim from further injury.

2. First aid – ascertain the condition of the casualty and the extent of any injuries. Administer first aid only if you know what you are doing. Make sure the victim is kept warm and reassured.

A warm drink will help, but ONLY if the person has been fully conscious throughout; never give alcohol.

- If a limb appears fractured, protect it from further movement.
- If the casualty is unconscious, check to see that he or she is breathing; if not, start artificial respiration immediately.
- Place the casualty in the recovery position: gently roll the person on to his or her side, head down to prevent choking.

3. Alert the nearest station personnel and/or the piste patrol/emergency services. Make a note of the name/number of the nearest piste marker.

4. Exchange names and contact details with all parties to the accident, including witnesses and station personnel.

5. Get the casualty to shelter as soon as it is safe to move them.

PICTURE CREDITS

The publisher would like to thank the following for permission to reproduce their photographs: **Office du Tourisme de Val d'Isère** - (Agence NUTS pp 15, 52, 108, 277, 280), (Mario Colonel pp 72, 157), (Christophe Guibbaud p 164); **Tignes Développement** p 22 - (Daniel Rousselot pp 173, 191, 220, 229, 238, 265, 266, 269), (Aril Toennessen p 224); **Sofia Barbas** p 24. Original piste map artwork by **Pierre Novat**.